ENDORSEMENTS

The biblical book of Revelation is a veritable metaphorical minefield, and so lends itself well to Roger VanDerWerken's interpretation as found in his new book *Captain's on the Bridge: The Book of Revelation from a Military Perspectivie.* VanDerWerken's book provides the reader an accessible, well-reasoned interpretation of the complex imagery of biblical Revelation arranged around contemporary militaristic language and themes.

Perhaps most significant to this work is VanDerWerken's ironical acknowledgment that the militaristic metaphorical language found in Revelation, while used to "recruit" Christians into service, purports a non-violent human resistance. The battle is the Lord's. VanDerWerken goes on to discuss the ideas of holy war, which he finds unacceptable, and just war, which he notes is undesirable, but sometimes necessary. Also emphasized are the cries for justice; God's unending patience; institutional evil, religion gone wrong, the interpretation of 666, as well as the eschatological hope for the day when war will cease.

Through detailed accounts of Iraqi and Kuwaiti missions, described by VanDerWerken, who is an officer and naval chaplain, he interprets some of Revelation's most vivid militaristic imagery. In the end, VanDerWerken makes clear the purposed message of John's Revelation: the call to a non-violent resistance of evil and the faithful worship of God.

VanDerWerken's book is a quick, reliable and easy read of some very complicated material.

— LeAnn Snow Flesher, PhD
Professor of Old Testament
American Baptist Seminary of the West at
The Graduate Theological Union
Berkeley, CA

Disclaimer from the start: Revelation has never been one of my favorite books of the Bible. The challenging imagery and some commentators' rather un-Christ-like confidence about what the future holds based on that imagery have often left me a bit cold. Roger VanDerWerken's unique approach is both refreshing and inviting. Using parallels with modern military language and practices, Chaplain VanDerWerken breathes new life and new perspective into some well-worn (perhaps even burned over?) territory. I especially like the fact that the approach taken is consistent with traditional Biblical analysis. Chaplain VanDerWerken keeps the Book of Revelation centered in the context of the larger whole of Holy Scripture, and does not attempt to use Revelation as the be-all or end-all of interpretation for the rest of the scriptural Canon. The result is a balanced, grounded study which is intriguing and highly enjoyable – even for reluctant readers like me!

— Chaplain Cameron Fish
United States Naval Academy

Captain's on the Bridge

The Book of Revelation from a Military Perspective

Roger VanDerWerken

Photos placed on the front cover, back cover, pages 54, 78, 132, and page 147 are used by permission of the US Navy. The views expressed in this book are solely those of the author. They do not necessarily represent the views of the United States Navy or the United States. The views expressed or implied in this work do not necessarily reflect those of Selah Publishing Group.

Scripture quotations in this commentary, unless otherwise indicated, are taken from the Holy Bible, New International Version ®. Copyright © 1973, 1978, 1984 by International Bible Society. Used by permission of Zondervan Publishing House. All rights reserved.

Copyright © 2007 by Roger VanDerWerken. All rights reserved.

Printed in the United States of America

Publishing services by Selah Publishing Group, LLC, Arizona.

No part of this publication may be reproduced, stored in a retrieval system or transmitted in any way by any means, electronic, mechanical, photocopy, recording or otherwise, without the prior permission of the author except as provided by USA copyright law.

ISBN: 978-1-58930-178-8
Library of Congress Control Number: 2006907908

For our struggle is not against flesh and blood …

Acknowledgements

Thanks to the following:

Thomas W. Blaine, Associate Professor, Ohio State University, for a friendship that dates to our time at the U.S. Naval Academy in the late 1970's. Our religious discussions have always been animated and enlightening.

LTCOL Michael Broihier, USMC; Associate Professor of Military Science at UC Berkeley for some really great ideas that have found their way into the text, and for keeping me honest with my military illustrations.

Captain Matt Chambliss, USMC, Alpha Company Commander, First Recruit Training Battalion, Recruit Training Regiment, Marine Corps Recruit Depot, San Diego, CA, for showing me the "ropes" at the Depot.

LeAnn Snow Flesher, Professor of Old Testament at the American Baptist Seminary of the West. Her course, Biblical Apocalyptic Literature, pointed out many of the literary similarities that the Book of Revelation holds in common with other writings of its day.

Lisa Fullam, Associate Professor of Ethics, Jesuit School of Theology in Berkeley, for advice, friendship, and profound insight into ethics, in general, and the war ethic, in particular.

Mr. Charles "Bud" Jermy, Jr., Dean of the Summer School and of Continuing Education at Cornell University, who urged me to declare boldly those things I held to be true while teaching the Book of Revelation at a church Bible study.

Master Gunnery Sergeant John Klimek, USMC, Staff Non-commissioned officer in charge of the RSS Oceanside, CA, for explaining the intricacies of Marine Corps Recruiting.

Lewis Mudge, Emeritus Professor of Theology, San Francisco Theological Seminary, for his course "Globalization, Ecumenism, and Ethics," which brought to light many of the activities of the sea and earth beasts in our modern world.

Professor Michael Nagler, founder of the Peace and Conflict Studies (PACS) Department at UC Berkeley, for his great insights into principled nonviolence. Even though I am using modern military imagery to describe the peace that unfolds in the Apocalypse, Professor Nagler would be quick to point out that the Book of Revelation does not allow us to assume that Jesus would accept modern warfare. His PACS 164 course ought to be required for anyone considering government service. E. Stanley Jones, the renowned Methodist missionary/evangelist to India once said that Nagler's hero, Mahatma Gandhi, showed him "more of the spirit of Christ than perhaps any other man in East or West."

Jean-Francois Racine, Assistant Professor of New Testament, Jesuit School of Theology in Berkeley, for a rigorous reading program involving just war theology, and for his cautions about exacerbating full-range military language and presenting a dualistic perspective about the world.

Hal Sanks, Professor of Systematic Theology, Jesuit School of Theology in Berkeley, for a course entitled "Clashing Symbols: Faith and Culture." Professor Sanks' teachings regarding the symbolic as something that "participates in and points us to God" were particularly helpful.

Chaplain Andrew Sholtes, LCDR, USN, for our many long, fruitful theological discussions, and for his proofreading. Andrew intimately understands the power of the sea beast, and has overcome him by the blood of the Lamb.

Professor Robert H. Smith, Professor of New Testament, Pacific Lutheran Theological Seminary in Berkeley, for his course, NT3516 The Apocalypse in Greek. He tenaciously kept me focused on the text of Revelation itself. Dr. Smith's *Apocalypse: A Commentary on Revelation in Words and Images* (The Liturgical Press, 2000) is one of the finest works I have read on the subject.

Acknowledgements

The Rev. Heng Sure, an American Buddhist monk who directs the Berkeley Buddhist Monastery, greatly encouraged me in this project. His class "With God on Our Side," taught at the Graduate Theological Union, helps students "analyze the roles of religion and spirituality in shaping men's and women's conviction to step aside from fighting and militarism and to seek alternatives to violence as a solution to conflict."

The Naval Chaplain candidates at the Chaplain School Basic course #99010 in Newport, Rhode Island – especially Chaplain Mike Weitecha, LT, USNR, and Rev. Brian Austring. Our theological debates were long, loud, and late into the evening.

The United States Navy Chaplain Corps (and the American public) for the vision to send its chaplains to post-graduate study, equipping us with the tools needed to "bear witness" to the United States Navy, a very powerful and necessary institution.

The faculty of the Westminster Theological Seminary in Philadelphia – professors Vern Poythress, and the late Ray Dillard, in particular – for getting me on the right path theologically.

Members and friends of the Memorial Baptist Church in Cortland, NY, for our Sunday Night Bible studies, and for a setting where we plowed through many of these ideas together.

My wife and best friend, Jacque, who keeps me honest, along with my three children, and other family members and friends so supportive of the work I do.

Any errors you may discover in this work – grammatical, theological or otherwise – are of my own doing, thank you very much.

Contents

ACKNOWLEDGEMENTS..7
PREFACE...13
INTRODUCTION..15

Chapter 1
   RECRUITING..31
      (Revelation 1:1-20)

Chapter 2
   BOOT CAMP..53
      (Revelation 2:1-3:22)

Chapter 3
   CAPTAIN'S ON THE BRIDGE..................................77
      (Revelation 4:1-5:14)

Chapter 4
   JUST CAUSE..89
      (Revelation 6:1-11)

Chapter 5
   SCHOOL CIRCLE...101
      (Rev. 7, 10, 13:9-10; 14:12-13; 15; 16:15; 20:1-6)

Chapter 6
   INTELLIGENCE ASSESSMENT..............................117
      (Rev. 11:1-6; 12; 13:1-8, 11-18; 14:1-5; 17; 19:11-16)

Chapter 7
    THE DAY OF THE LORD (ARMAGEDDON)..........................139
       (Rev. 6:12-17; 8-9; 11-14; 16; 18; 19:17-21; 20:7-10)

Chapter 8
    THE WAR TRIBUNAL & A LASTING PEACE..........................161
       (Revelation 20:11-22:6)

Epilogue
    AND OLD TALES BE RETOLD...169
       (Revelation 22:7-21)

APPENDICES..171
BIBLIOGRAPHY...175
ABOUT THE AUTHOR..179

Preface

Throughout my career as a minister (ten years as a church pastor, and nine as a chaplain in the United States Navy), people have frequently asked for my thoughts concerning the Book of Revelation, and what the future of our world might entail. There is an enormous interest in the study of last things. I have found that Bible studies are packed whenever the subject is addressed, and participation is animated. One of the reasons is that the Book of Revelation, or the Apocalypse, describes a military campaign, but it is one that is far different from any armed conflict this world has ever seen. The book speaks of war, but it is God who wages it, and the enemies are not human. There is a peace that results, but it is one that is eternal, never again to be shattered. Most human wars have been fought with the claim that "God is on our side." In this one, the question is rather, "Are we on God's side?"[1] Those who choose to follow the great General[2] revealed in this book are promised peace – a peace that is first of all internal, one that calms our souls in the midst of a chaotic world, but it is also one that comes at the end of days, ridding our world of evil and chaos forever. The purpose of Revelation is neither to polarize the human community nor to paint a gloomy picture of despair. Despite all of the warlike

---

[1] Attributed to Abraham Lincoln during the American Civil War. Available from http:// www.leaderu.com/offices/stoll/news4-96.html; Internet.

[2] Throughout Scripture, the Biblical authors used many metaphors attempting to capture the greatness of God – God as Father, Mother, Husband, Judge, or Farmer among the more significant. In this work, I am using the metaphor of Warrior, because it is the image that best captures the unfolding events of the Book of Revelation.

images, the Great King[3] revealed in the Book of Revelation offers hope to all who follow. In joining His Army, we become courageous peacemakers, extending that hope to others.

My goal is to write pastorally, and my intended audiences are those who desire to make some sort of sense out of the Book of Revelation but have had little or no formal theological training. *Captain's on the Bridge* should also prove very helpful to pastors and church leaders entrusted with leading the people of God. Military veterans and men and women currently serving on Active Duty may find this work of great interest as well. If I am able to contribute even a smidgeon to the reader's understanding of one of the greatest books in Scripture, or cause someone to place his or her faith in the great God who is revealed in it, the energy expended on this project will be worth the effort.

My credentials are certainly no better than those who have gone before me. I am not a scholar by any stretch of the imagination, but perhaps my experiences as a Naval Officer and military chaplain may offer a different set of lenses through which the reader might view the text.

---

[3] Traditional Christian theology would refer to the Great King as "God, the Father." I also refer Him as "God," or "the Most High."

Introduction

Military men and women understand that we live in a world where there is much evil. The way in which we live often results in terrorism, international acts of aggression, and armed conflict. In response, the armed forces of most nations are highly vigilant. In the United States, even during times of peace, there are Aircraft Carrier Strike Groups and Marine Corps Expeditionary Strike Groups deployed from both coasts, keeping international sea-lanes open. The Army and the Air Force maintain perpetual watch over national security, while the Coast Guard protects our coastal and inland waterways. Military men and women, in every command, from many countries, train to fight and win their nations' wars.

Christians (and there are many who serve in the armed forces) are also involved in warfare, but it is nonviolent in nature; it is a spiritual struggle for the souls of men and women who are made in the image of God, and one that is designed to permeate and improve the structures of society. The Book of Revelation suggests that we battle against an enemy who is insidious and seems omnipresent. A dragon, bent on making war against *"those who obey God's commandments and hold to the testimony of Jesus"* (12:17), is our primary nemesis. One of his lieutenants is a beast, rising out of the sea, who seeks to *"make war against the saints and to conquer them"* (13:7). Yet another beast, rising from the earth, makes *"its inhabitants worship the first beast (13:12).*[4] Spiritual battles have

---

[4]These enemies go by other names, as well: the dragon is also referred to as "Satan," "the serpent," or "the devil" (12:9); the sea beast is also known as "the scarlet beast" (17:3) or "the beast" (19:20); and the earth beast also goes by "the great harlot (17:1), or "the false prophet" (19:20).

been raging since the time of Adam and Eve; they torment us now, and will continue to flare up until all of the events described in the Book of Revelation have unfolded.

Coming against the red dragon and his minions is the Lord Jesus Christ.[5] He does the fighting (17:14), and *"with justice he judges and makes war"* (19:11). His Army has two major components: a heavenly division, made up of an unseen multitude of angels who follow Him into battle (17:14; 19:14); and an earthly division made up of human beings who place their trust in His leadership. This earthly division, or the Church,[6] made up of thousands of smaller units, including the seven to whom Revelation was first written (chaps. 2-3), has the primary responsibility of proclaiming the good news of the kingdom of God while, at the same time, resisting the two beasts allied to the dragon. (In chapter six, we shall learn that the sea beast is a symbol for human government gone wrong, while the earth beast is a system of perverted religion that seeks to coerce humankind into worshiping the State.) Unlike the weapons of earthly armies, the weapons of the Church are spiritual. We do not use guns, missiles, or bombs; but light, hope, and peace. These are divine in nature, capable of demolishing enemy strongholds (2 Cor. 10:4). We clothe ourselves with the armor of light (Rom. 13:12); we love, we forgive, and we show mercy. Our tactics go for the heart, and throw the enemy off balance.

In the same way as a soldier trusts the wisdom and tactics of his or her commanding general, or as a sailor trusts his or her captain to engage the warship, Christian soldiers are exhorted to trust the leadership of the Heavenly General portrayed in the Book of Revelation. There is, however, one crucial difference: earthly generals make tactical errors, and the outcome of any given war is never certain. In the battle that rages for human souls, the Lord Jesus

---

[5]Throughout the text, I will be referring to our Lord as "the General," "the Great Warrior," or "the Commander." He is also "the male child" (12:5), "the rider on the white horse" (19:11), and quite paradoxically, "the Lamb" (5:6),

[6]Whenever I refer to believers in any era, from any denomination, I will be using an upper case "C" to spell the word "Church." Whenever I speak of local bodies of believers, denominationally specific, who meet together for worship, evangelism, etc., I will make use of the lower case.

Introduction

Christ has already triumphed (5:5) – there is an inner peace for all who will follow – and He will triumph (17:14); there is a final peace yet to come. Those who follow Christ are guaranteed victory, while those who wage war against Him will be *"thrown alive into the fiery lake of burning sulfur"* (19:20; 20:15).

There are many frightening images in this book which sear our conscience: those who worship the beast will *"drink of the wine of God's fury"* and will be *"tormented with burning sulfur in the presence of the holy angels and of the Lamb"* (14:10). Others are trampled in the great winepress of God's wrath (14:19), while still more gnaw their tongues in agony, and curse the God of heaven (16:11). Angels cry out to the birds: *"Come, gather together for the great supper of God, so that you may eat the flesh of kings, generals, and mighty men, of horses and their riders, and the flesh of all people, free and slave, small and great"* (19:17-18). Some of these judgments sound hauntingly familiar to the random destruction that takes place on modern battlefields, but with God, the destruction is not random; it is very precise. His servants will not be harmed (7:3), even as those forces that inflict injustice and evil upon the human community are destroyed.

The Book of Revelation is meant to inspire hope for the believer in Jesus Christ. No matter how dire our earthly situations, no matter how great the injustices, God is with His people. He protects us, and will one day bring us into His kingdom. In the mean time, "the servant of God ... is an enlisted man obeying the orders of his king."[7] We are to occupy the territory God has given us until He returns for it (Luke 19:13, KJV). Out of respect for the Heavenly General who has already granted victory, we keep His commands (3:10) – the greatest of which are to love God and our neighbor (Matt. 22:37-39); we persevere and endure hardship (2:3); we remain vigilant (3:2; 16:15), properly armed (16:15; cf. Eph. 6:10-18), and with patient endurance (13:10) follow Him wherever He goes (14:4).

---

[7] Vernard Eller, *War and Peace from Genesis to Revelation* (Scottdale, PA; Kitchener, Ontario: Herald Press, 1981), 156.

Principles of interpretation
There are many different ways in which one can interpret the Book of Revelation. Most fall into one of three categories: the *predictive*, the *historical*, or the *idealist*. The predictive approach reads the text as a "transcript of future historical events."[8] The beast that rises out of the sea (13:1), for example, is understood to be the Antichrist, a man who will arise at some point in the future and deceive the entire world. Over the course of history, many interpreters of Revelation have offered predictions that have proven embarrassingly inaccurate. We will note a few of these in the course of our study, and illustrate some of the fundamental weaknesses of this approach. Revelation "was not written to predict particular historical events two thousand years in the future of its original author and audience."[9] Nevertheless, there are elements that await future fulfillment. We do not yet, for example, live in a world where there is "*no more death or mourning or crying or pain*" (21:4).

The historical approach reads the text as a "commentary on political events and figures of the author's own time."[10] The original audience would have understood the symbolism as "fluently" as modern readers understand the elephant or the donkey when engaged in contemporary political discussion. So to interpret the text of Revelation, we must first decode the symbols and then discover the first century personnel involved. For many historical interpreters, the beast rising out of the sea (13:1) was the emperor Nero, a great persecutor of the Church. But there are two significant problems for those who take this approach: 1) if everything in Revelation refers to events that happened 2,000 years ago, the question of relevancy arises for the 21st century reader, and 2) many of the symbols clearly refer to future events – the ideal state described in chapter twenty-one, chief among them.

---

[8]Richard B. Hays, *The Moral Vision of the New Testament: Community, Cross, New Creation: A Contemporary Introduction to New Testament Ethics* (United States of America: HarperSanFrancisco, 1996), 170.
[9]Ibid., 171.
[10]Ibid., 172.

Introduction

The idealist approach maintains that the text of Revelation "sets out in poetic form certain theological conceptions. It is not particularly concerned with the situation of the early church, nor with that of the church in later days, nor with that of the end-time. It simply sets out principles on which God acts throughout human history. This secures its relevance for all periods of the church's history. But its refusal to see a firm historical anchorage seems to most students dubious to say the least."[11] The beast that rises out of the sea (13:1), in this case, may be understood as a symbol for repressive governments that usurp for themselves the authority that only belongs to Almighty God. These rear up their ugly heads generation after generation.

As Morris suggests, "It seems that elements from more than one of these views are required for a satisfactory understanding of Revelation."[12] There was a historical audience to whom this book was directed, but it has also provided hope to believers in Jesus Christ throughout the centuries, and it seems that there are numerous elements that must be assigned to the future.

Five more principles
There are five additional principles of interpretation that will aid our understanding of the Book of Revelation: 1) it is a book that is inspired by God; 2) its main purpose is to bring the reader/hearer into a relationship with Jesus Christ, and maintain fidelity to Him; 3) there is an extensive use of symbols; 4) some of the action has already taken place while some has not yet transpired (the already/not yet); and 5) the author employs the principle of "flashback."

---

[11]Leon Morris, *The Revelation of St. John: An Introduction and Commentary* (Grand Rapids, Michigan: William B. Eerdmans Publishing Company, 1978), 18.
[12]Ibid.

Inspiration
As with every book in Sacred Scripture, we believe that the Book of Revelation is a work inspired by God (n. 2 Tim. 3:16-17; 2 Pet. 1:20-21). The Vatican II Council of the Roman Catholic Church reaffirmed its traditional teaching on inspiration with the following definition:

> "Those divinely revealed realities which are contained and presented in sacred Scripture have been committed to writing under the inspiration of the Holy Spirit." God made use of the powers and abilities of chosen authors so that "with him acting in them and through them, they, as true authors, consigned to writing everything and only those things that he wanted."[13]

This is a statement with which most Christians can find agreement. Although very few books of the New Testament claim inspiration,[14] the Apocalypse is one that does. Its very first verse declares that the ensuing work is, *"The revelation of Jesus Christ"* (1:1). In studying the words of this great book, and in asking questions as we struggle to make sense of its images, we exercise humility. We are reading an inspired work; we do not trifle with its contents, but surrender to its authority. Near the end of this masterpiece, John adds (and this, too, is inspired):

---

[13] Raymond E. Brown, Joseph A. Fitzmyer, and Roland E. Murphy, eds., *The New Jerome Bible Handbook* (Collegeville, MN: The Liturgical Press, 1992), 321.

[14] The authoritative writings which ultimately made their way into the New Testament were included because of their: 1) apostolicity – the source of their authority came from apostolic tradition (i.e. the teachings of the apostles), 2) catholicity – relevant to the church as a whole, 3) orthodoxy – molded by the faith tradition (the Scriptures were written long after Christian communities were founded, and 4) traditional usage. Self-claimed inspiration was not a criterion for inclusion. See Harry Y. Gamble, *The New Testament Canon: Its Making and Meaning* (Philadelphia: Fortress Press, 1985), 67-72.

Introduction

> *I warn everyone who hears the words of the prophecy of this book: If anyone adds anything to them, God will add to him the plagues described in this book. And if anyone takes words away from this book of prophecy, God will take away from him his share in the tree of life and in the holy city, which are described in this book* (Rev. 22:18-19; cf. Deut. 4:2; Prov. 30:5-6; Gal. 1:8-9).

This principle affirms that God is the source of inspiration for the books of the Old and New Testaments, but He employed frail human authors (scattered over a 1500 year period, using three different languages) who were embedded in very specific cultural settings. The context out of which the Book of Revelation arose is very important. There is continuity in Scripture (large segments of Matthew 24, for example, are very similar to Revelation), obliging us to read the Apocalypse in connection with the rest of the Bible. Progressive revelation, the concept that Scripture revealed later in human history unfolds more of God's Divine plan for humanity than does earlier material, is also an important dynamic.[15]

Christocentricity

Jesus Christ is the focus of the Book of Revelation. Its opening and closing thoughts mention His name, and the most powerful appeal of the book, found near the end of the last chapter, invites the reader/hearer to develop a relationship with Him:

> *The Spirit and the bride say, "Come!" And let him who hears say, "Come!" Whoever is thirsty, let him come; and whoever wishes, let him take the free gift of the water of life* (22:17).

The thrilling scenes of the lion from the tribe of Judah entering the throne room of God (5:5), and of the rider on the white horse returning in glorious conquest (19:11), are centerpieces. As taught in every New Testament book, we are commanded to follow Him

---

[15]Many Christians have a handy saying for Biblical interpretation: "The New (Testament) is in the Old concealed; the Old is in the New revealed."

(cf. Luke 24:44; John 5:39-40; 2 Cor. 1:20; Heb. 1:1-3). To embrace Christ is to embrace life; to reject Him is to perish. Jesus came to die for our sins and to offer us peace with God. Christians in Smyrna are encouraged to *"be faithful, even to the point of death"* (2:10); those in Pergamum are complimented for having remained true to his name (2:13); the Philadelphians receive praise for not denying his name (3:8). Revelation teaches, *"The kingdom of the world has become the kingdom of our Lord and of his Christ, and he will reign for ever and ever"* (11:15), and that *"The time has come for ... rewarding ... those who reverence your name ... and for destroying those who destroy the earth"* (11:18). Wisdom dictates that those who do not wish to undergo the judgments of Revelation will follow Him who offers protection from them (n. Matt. 10:28).

The use of symbols
In Revelation 1:1 we read the words: "He made it known." This expression is taken from the Greek "semaino" which means "to indicate or signify." The noun form "semeion" is often translated as "miracle, sign, token, or wonder." One could translate the passage as: "through the use of signs (or symbols) God has communicated." The word is used frequently in the New Testament. Some of the more interesting passages include:

> "A wicked and adulterous generation asks for a miraculous <u>sign</u>" (Matt. 12:38-39).

> "These <u>signs</u> shall will accompany those who believe: In my name they will drive out demons; they will speak in new tongues; they will pick up snakes with their hands; and when they drink deadly poison, it will not hurt them at all" (Mark 16:17-18).

> "'But I, when I am lifted up from the earth, will draw all men to myself.' He said this to <u>show</u> what kind of death he was going to die' (John 12:32-33).

Introduction

> "And in these days came prophets from Jerusalem unto Antioch. And there stood up one of them named Agabus, and <u>signified</u> by the Spirit that there should be great dearth throughout all the world" (Acts 11:27-28, KJV; cf. Acts 21:11).

Symbols are employed frequently in the United States military. When a guidon is passed from one officer to the next, it is a symbol of the transfer of power. When a helmet and boots are placed on a wooden cross, we know that a comrade has died. When the flag is hoisted to the masthead of a United States Ship, a symbol proclaiming the values of the nation is prominently displayed for all to view.

The Book of Revelation is filled with signs and symbols. There are lampstands, seals and plagues. There is a dragon, and beasts that rise out of sea and earth. There is a woman clothed with the sun, and another who holds a cup filled with abominable things. Fascinating symbolic numbers are found throughout: 144,000; 1260; 666; time, times and half a time; one thousand years. The number seven is used 31 times. Some of the symbols are defined for us: the seven lampstands are seven churches (1:20), and the dragon is Satan (12:9). Most, however, are left undefined, requiring the reader to call out for wisdom as he or she struggles to interpret (13:18; 17:9).

In taking things "literally," we often miss the power of that which is being communicated. It is a mistake, for example, to take the word "hour," in *"the hour of trial that is going to come upon the whole world"* (3:10), and assume that the author is speaking about sixty minutes. The expression "ten days," in the phrase *"you will suffer persecution for ten days,"* (2:10) is symbolic. We do not expect a literal chain to bind the Devil in the Abyss for a thousand years (20:1-2), nor is the amount of blood flowing out of the winepress of God's wrath plausible (14:20). As we read the Book of Revelation, we expect to find signs and symbols that point to things that are far greater. Wisdom, indeed, is a necessary ingredient in interpreting the text.

The "Already/Not Yet"
The spiritual warfare described in the Apocalypse is already happening, but it is not yet over. In chapter one, for example, John tells his audience that, *"On the Lord's Day I was in the Spirit"* (1:10). The phrase "on the Lord's Day" is equivalent to the Old Testament "Day of the Lord," an expression that often implied great catastrophe, used frequently to refer to the end of the world (n. Isa. 13; 24; Ezek. 7; Joel 2). The prophet Joel's use of the term is of particular interest because the Apostle Peter declared that it was fulfilled on Pentecost Sunday:

> *"I will pour out my Spirit on all people. Your sons and daughters will prophesy, your old men will dream dreams, your young men will see visions... I will show wonders in the heavens and on the earth, blood and fire and billows of smoke. The sun will be turned to darkness and the moon to blood before the coming of the great and dreadful day of the LORD"* (Joel 2:28-31; cf. Acts 2:16).

To be sure, the outpouring of God's Spirit occurred on Pentecost, but the cosmic upheaval to which Joel referred did not. In using the expression "on the Lord's Day," John writes to those who have "already" experienced the Pentecost event – members of the seven churches (chaps. 2-3) – but as the text unfolds, he also offers his audience a description of the "not yet" sections of Joel's prophecy. Christians believe these events accompany the Second Coming of Jesus Christ.

The words of Revelation 1:19 add to the "already/not yet" argument: *"Write, therefore, what you have seen, what is now and what will take place later."* Many commentators think that this passage refers to three periods of time, past, present, and future, but others suggest that the divisions of verse nineteen are actually twofold.[16] From this point of view, the proper way of reading verse nineteen would be: 'Write, therefore, what you have seen: 1) the

---
[16] Robert H. Mounce, *The Book of Revelation* (Grand Rapids, Michigan: William B. Eerdmans Publishing Company, 1977), 81-82.

things that are – "the already" – the inner peace available to all who would follow, and 2) what will take place later – the "not yet" – the eschatological peace that is coming.' For the purposes of our study, we will refer to the "not yet" part of the battle as "the Day of the Lord."

In war, there are often major turning points where combatants know that the outcome has already been decided, even though battles still rage. There may be a significant span of time between D-Day and final liberation, but the end result is certain. This is how we should read the Book of Revelation. The people of God have already experienced victory, but final liberation – the Day of the Lord – is yet to come.

Flashback[17]
Warriors who have gone through traumatic experiences often reencounter those scenarios in their minds' eye. Certain sights, sounds, or even the weather may trigger trauma. The Book of Revelation is not written in chronological order. As good writers often do, part of the story is told, and then the reader is "flashed back" to an earlier scenario in order to be given better insight. We see this frequently in Revelation. Seal number six, for example, tells us that "*The sun turned black*" (6:12), while the fourth trumpet mentions that "*a third of the sun was struck ... A third of the day was without light*" (8:12). This does not mean that somewhere between (6:12) and (8:12) the sun started shining again (a chronological point of view would require this); it means we journey back to a previous mention of the catastrophic cosmic event. Other examples of flashback include: the second trumpet (8:8) where "*a third of the sea was turned into blood,*" revisited in (16:3) where the angel "*poured out his bowl on the sea, and it turned into blood;*" and the sixth seal (6:14) where "*every mountain and island was removed from its place,*" revisited in (16:20) where "*every is-*

---

[17]Most theologians prefer the term "recapitulation" to describe this principle. I prefer the term "flashback," because it is the term employed by military personnel to describe the phenomena.

land fled away and the mountains could not be found." We shall encounter many such examples of this principle as we read through the Book of Revelation.

War and the Christian faith
Theologians have outlined three different positions held by the Christian Church and by nation states as they consider appropriate responses to evil and/or international aggression: 1) nonviolent resistance, 2) just war, and 3) holy war.

Human wars are sad, tragic affairs. Some Christians are convinced that war is always wrong, and that it is never appropriate to use violence. Men such as Dr. Martin Luther King, Jr. in the United States, and the Hindu Mahatma Gandhi in India, were able to defeat the evils of racial segregation and imperialism through nonviolent means. There are Christian scholars who suggest that the Book of Revelation is a manual for nonviolent resistance. Hays, for example, points out that the image of "the Lamb that was slaughtered," used twenty-eight times in Revelation, is a picture of God overcoming the world, not "through a show of force but through the suffering and death of Jesus." He also suggests that by placing this Lamb at the center of heaven's praise and worship, one can hardly "validate violence and coercion." "Those who destroy the earth," he says, will eventually be destroyed (11:18; cf. Matt. 26:52), but that will happen on God's time. The Book of Revelation does not "constitute a program for human military action." In chapter thirteen, he suggests, the reader will note a clarion call to nonviolence:

> *"He who has an ear, let him hear. If anyone is to go into captivity, into captivity he will go. If anyone is to be killed with the sword, with the sword he will be killed. This calls for patient endurance and faithfulness on the part of the saints"* (13:9-10).[18]

Other Christians believe that the only true peace will come about at the end of time, by God's action. There may be occasions when the use of physical violence is needed to defend one's neighbor and

---
[18]Hays, 174, 175, 178 passim.

to stop evil. Police and military forces are established by the State to prevent individuals from taking justice into their own hands (n. Rom. 13:1-5), and there are many Christians who sense a calling to serve in professions where the use of force is justified. Those who do so, in a way that is compatible with Christian morality, are willing, if necessary, even to take the lives of others for principles such as justice, liberty, and the welfare of the State. They do so out of love for neighbor and for country, not because they love war or enjoy violence and destruction. They submit themselves to a highly disciplined structure of moral accountability, and rely upon the wisdom of government leaders, those to whom the use of force has been entrusted. Although the Book of Revelation addresses neither "just" war nor the military profession, there are hints in other parts of the New Testament. John the Baptist (Luke 3:14), the Apostle Peter (Acts 10), and Jesus (Matt. 8:10) each had significant conversations with military personnel; none suggested that the profession is inappropriate, and in Jesus' encounter, His commendation of the centurion's faith was particularly noteworthy – and our Lord was not known to mince words where sin was involved (n. Matt. 15:7; 23:13-15; John 8:11).

Tragically, there have been many Christians throughout history who have used the Book of Revelation to justify the extermination of their enemies. Holy war, practiced in the earlier eras of the Old Testament, is not an option for the believer. Neither human beings nor nation states are completely evil or completely good; all are in need of redemption. There is no such entity as an infallible crusader of truth, and God does not take sides.[19] Our ultimate enemy is not flesh and blood; he is spiritual. One factor that modern-day "crusaders" tend to ignore is that Old Testament holy war was often directed *against* the nation of Israel because of sins committed against God (n. Exod. 32:27-28; Judg. 20:35). The question to be posed is not whether God is on our side, but rather, "are we are on

---

[19]In his second inaugural address, given in the midst of the Civil War, President Lincoln agonized: "Both (sides) read the same Bible and pray to the same God, and each invoked His aid against the other ... The prayers of both could not be answered. That of neither has been answered fully. The Almighty has His own purposes."

God's side?" Church-era military ventures, launched with crusade-like zeal – such as the removal of the "infidel" from sites in the Holy Land, the Puritan Revolution of the 17th century, and genocide against Native Americans – are among the saddest chapters in human history.

In human warfare the issues are never black and white; often both sides claim "just cause." One's enemies are neither completely evil – we never battle against "the Great Satan" – nor are one's allies perfectly holy. Human war will never bring about a perfect world; we are incapable of waging a "war to end all wars." The purpose of this book is not to glorify human war. The examples of contemporary warfare you discover in the text (and I use U.S. military examples only because I am familiar with them) serve only to illustrate the spiritual war unfolding in the Book of Revelation, a war directed against the red dragon and two hideous beasts that rise out of earth and sea. It is not a war against flesh and blood.

The ancient prophets of Israel envisioned one final battle, at the end of time, when the Lord would bring victory. The "Day of the Lord" – mentioned in Isaiah chapters 13 and 24, Ezekiel chapter 7, and Joel chapter 2 – was to be an event of pure war, waged by God, for the salvation of Israel. At that time, God would triumph over all evil, and peace would come, never again to be broken. Unfolding in the Book of Revelation is a description of what the prophets had so long ago envisioned, the fulfillment of the Day of the Lord.

The metaphors in the Book of Revelation are often so graphic (conjuring up horrible human wars) that we recoil at their very mention. But we need to remember that it is God who wages this war; it is spiritual in nature, and it will be the last one our world will ever know. As we journey together through the twenty-two chapters of this extraordinary book – and we are told that everyone who reads is blessed (1:3) – what will unfold before our minds' eye is a war, with depictions of violence beyond our wildest imagination. The promise of Revelation is that all who place their faith in the God who wages this war will be granted victory. The war and violence depicted in the Apocalypse will culminate in a peaceable kingdom, a state in which God will wipe every tear from our eyes, where *"there will be no more death or mourning or crying or pain, for the old order of things has passed away"* (21:4).

In Summary
By way of summary, this interpretation of the Book of Revelation suggests that it can be understood best by using the metaphor of a modern military operation, read in context with the rest of Holy Scripture. The Lord Jesus Christ, allied with His angelic army, engages spiritual forces of evil that afflict our world. On a human level, those who follow Jesus are called to resist the beasts that rise out of earth and sea, and share the good news of God's kingdom with others. The words of this great book were applicable to Christians in the past, have great meaning for us today, and will continue to impact the lives of believers, in significant and powerful ways, long into the future. The reader will encounter numerous signs and symbols, all which ultimately proclaim the power and glory of Almighty God. In reading Revelation, much of what is written has "already" taken place, while significant sections have "not yet" transpired. The text employs frequent use of "flashback" to enlighten us further concerning the judgment of God.

This work is not meant to be an "in-depth" verse-by-verse study of the last book of the Bible. For that, I would recommend any of the commentaries listed in the bibliography. My approach is more thematic, suggesting that Revelation unveils a war plan, carried out by the Creator of heaven and earth, resulting in victory over the spiritual forces of evil that ravage our world. A rider on a white horse, promising a new heaven and a new earth, leads the armies of heaven. An enormous red dragon, whose destination is a lake of burning sulfur, heads up the opposition. By placing our faith in Jesus Christ, we are ensured victory. Together with John, the scribe of the Apocalypse, we seek – through peaceful means – to recruit, equip and deploy spiritual warriors who will serve in the Lamb's Army. We begin first with a sobering assessment of the struggle that goes on within each of us, but we also seek to win the hearts and minds of all who are made in the image of God. In reflecting upon the terrible judgments described in the Book of Revelation, we take comfort that this final war is not against flesh and blood, but against spiritual forces that seek to separate us from the love of God.

Chapter 1

RECRUITING

(Revelation 1:1-20)

"Come, Follow me," Jesus said, "and I will make you fishers of men."
   - Matthew 4:19

The revelation of Jesus Christ ... (v. 1)
"Will you sign up in the greatest Army this world has ever known?" The opening verses of Revelation chapter one almost beg the question. Let your mind wander a bit. Imagine a cosmic recruiting office staffed by a man named John who is receiving orders from higher command. As he tells the story, you are invited to join.

The word "revelation" comes from the Greek "apocalypse", which means, "the unveiling of things that are hidden." Christ, our General, shows God's servants *"what must soon take place."* Ultimately, that which is revealed is a massive military operation, waged against repressive powers of darkness that seek to destroy the souls of human beings made in the image of God. The unfolding campaign is one that Christ personally leads, and from which He and all of His followers emerge victorious.

The astute reader will note that this is the revelation of Jesus Christ; it is neither "The Revelation of St. John the Divine," nor is it the "Book of Revelation s." The revelation (note that the noun is singular) comes from God, who gave it to Jesus Christ. Jesus relayed the message by sending an angel to his servant John. John, in turn, speaks to us, by writing it down. In essence, there is a recruiting "chain of command." The revelation goes from God to Jesus, from Jesus to an angel, from an angel to John, and from John to the servants of God.

Blessed… are those who hear… and take to heart… (v. 3)
Military recruiters offer wonderful benefits for those who join. Educational opportunities, medical and dental coverage, and a retirement pension after twenty years of service are among the most significant. The finest soldiers, however, serve because they believe in the values of their country; they want to be affiliated with an organization that values pride, integrity, and courage; and they want to give back to a nation that has given so much to them. They serve because they are contributing to a cause bigger than themselves. The benefits are an added blessing.

As the reader or hearer absorbs the words of the Apocalypse, a challenge is issued: *"the time is near."* Are you ready to follow the One about whom this book is written? Do you believe the things that are spoken of Him? Do you cherish the values for which He stands? Do you want to affiliate with others who serve in His Army? If you take to heart the things that are in this prophecy, if you honor Him with your life, the blessings of abundant life, peace, and joy will follow.

The words of this verse are in the present tense. The promises of blessing were available to the very first readers and hearers, but they also applied to Christians throughout the ages, and to us today in our struggle against evil. You will be encouraged as you read the words of the Apocalypse, hear them faithfully preached, and apply them to your life.

John … (v. 4)
Recruiters are experienced veterans who understand how the military works; they know its trials and rigors, as well as its benefits and joys. Often, those serving on recruiting duty would rather be somewhere else. Bringing others into the fold is very hard work. Recruiting involves people skills, and it entails long hours and much

salesmanship. Recruiters often serve in areas where there is little familiarity with the armed forces, or even in places where there is great animosity towards those who would bring their sons and daughters into the profession of arms.

Christ selected John to be a recruiter for His Army. There is considerable scholarly debate as to whom this is,[20] but for the purposes of our work, we will simply refer to him as "John." In three other places within the text, the author identifies himself, always with the same power and simplicity (1:1, 9; 22:8).

To the seven churches in the province of Asia ... (v. 4)
Recruiters are assigned to geographic regions. The United States Marine Corps, for example, has six recruiting districts that cover the continental United States, Alaska, Hawaii, and all overseas territories. Local high schools are the main source for the young men and women who would join. Occasionally, there is a high school principal who willingly cooperates with the recruiter. In areas where such cooperation exists, the recruiter might send a letter, asking for a list of graduating seniors. He or she will then contact each of the seniors to ascertain if there is interest in serving. More often, however, the principal is not your "pal," and more subtle ways of making contact must be developed (n. Matt. 10:16).

Churches are responsible for recruiting warriors for the Lord's Army, so in this case, John sends a letter to seven churches that had been established in large Roman cities along a prominent trading route in the province of Asia Minor (modern day Turkey). The cities in which these churches were located – Ephesus, Smyrna, Pergamum, Thyatira, Sardis, Philadelphia, and Laodicea – were "roughly thirty to fifty miles apart along a circular road that went north to Pergamum, turned southeast to Laodicea, and returned full circle to Ephesus through the valley of the Maeander."[21] Those

---

[20] Most conservative scholars believe this to be the Apostle. Other suggestions include: 1) an unknown "Elder John" who resided in Ephesus, 2) the intentional use of a pseudonym, or 3) or an equally unsubstantiated "John the Prophet."
[21] Mounce, 27.

who worshiped in these cities were the first recipients of God's revelation, but Christians believe the intended audience is much larger.

[22]Vernard Eller, *The Most Revealing Book of the Bible: Making Sense out of Revelation* (Grand Rapids: William Eerdmans Publishing Company, 1974), 45.

"Seven," a number that speaks of perfection or completion,[23] is the first of many symbols found in the text. It may be, as John writes to the seven churches of Asia Minor, that the principle of divine inspiration points to an audience far greater. The symbolic nature of the number seven suggests that the Book of Revelation is addressed to the "universal" Church – She who transcends time and denomination. The exhortations that we are about to read apply just as much to us as to the original recipients. Recruitment for the Lord's Army extends to all people in every era.

Grace and peace to you … (v. 4)
The Great Warrior, for whom John and all Christians recruit, extends greetings. He offers us a way out of our sinful condition. In the midst of ongoing spiritual warfare, He proposes peace.

Grace, often defined as "unmerited favor," is a gift. Young men and women who have no money, no chance at a formal education, or no role models in their lives can often find a sense of purpose in the armed forces. Through military service, the government offers a way for many to rise above their poverty-stricken situations. In a far more significant way, the great God of heaven extends unmerited favor to all. Instead of death, Christ offers life; instead of despair, there is hope; instead of fear, love.

---

[23] Throughout the Bible, the number "seven" serves as a symbol of completeness, perfection or fullness. God created the heavens and the earth in seven days (Gen. 2:2-3). Jesus said we must forgive each other *"seventy-seven times"* (Matt. 18:22). The seventh day, the seventh week, and the seventh month were all holy to the Old Testament Jew. Jubilees occur at the close of forty-nine years – seven times seven years (Lev. 25:10). In the Book of Revelation, there are seven spirits (1:4); seven golden lampstands (1:12); seven stars (1:16); seven blazing lamps (4:5); seven seals (5:1); a Lamb with seven horns and seven eyes (5:6); seven angels holding seven trumpets (8:2); seven thunders (10:4); seven thousand people (11:13); a dragon with seven heads and seven crowns (12:3); a beast with seven heads (13:1) which are seven hills (17:9) and also seven kings (17:10); and seven angels given seven vials containing seven plagues (15:6-7).

Peace always involves justice. As Dr. Martin Luther King, Jr. said, "Injustice anywhere is a threat to justice everywhere."[24] Those, such as Dr. King, who practice nonviolence, seek to rectify injustice through peaceful resistance. When a nation makes the agonizing decision to go to war, one of the many factors it must consider is "right intent," that of establishing a just peace. The peace that God extends is one that is just; it was established at the cross when Christ died for our sins. So in the opening verses of the Apocalypse, our General offers peace right now, "*with God through our Lord Jesus Christ*" (Rom. 5:1), but He also offers a peace that is yet to come, when He will "*wipe every tear from* (our) *eyes*" (21:4).

From him who is, and who was, and who is to come… (v. 4)
The earthly general commands for two or three years; the Heavenly King for whom John recruits is eternal. He has always existed; He lives now, and will always reign over the heavens and the earth. Many times in Scripture and throughout the Book of Revelation (4:8; 5:13; 11:17; 21:6) we read of His timeless nature. The Divine name given to Moses in the Old Testament (Exod. 3:14) means, "The Being One," the One who always is. God is beyond time. He knows the end from the beginning. The Psalmist writes "*a thousand years in your sight are like a day that has just gone by, or like a watch in the night*" (90:4). The concept of time as we know it will be an unknown quantity in the world that is to come.

from the seven spirits before his throne … (v. 4)
The expression "*seven spirits of God*" is used three times in the Book of Revelation (3:1; 4:5; 5:6). Some understand this as a reference to the Holy Spirit. Isaiah 11:2, for example, refers to the seven-fold nature of the Spirit of the Lord. The term "*seven spirits*" is in the middle of a phrase coupling together "*from him who is and who was, and who is to come*" (v. 4) with "*Jesus Christ, who is the faithful witness*" (v. 5). This phrase would then speak to the triune nature of our God – Father, Holy Spirit, and Son – the Holy Trinity.

---

[24] Martin Luther King, Jr., "Letter from Birmingham Jail," April 16, 1963, available from http:// www.quotationspage.com/quote/24974.html; Internet.

Others suggest that the seven spirits may be the heavenly reality behind the seven-branch lampstand that stood before the Holy of Holies in the ancient temple. The sanctuary of old was "*a copy and shadow of what is in heaven*" (Heb. 8:5). If the cherubim who hovered above the Ark of the Covenant in the old tabernacle (Exod. 25:18-20) are representations of heavenly beings (Ezek. 1:5-9; Isa. 6:2-3; Rev. 4:6-8), perhaps the lampstands are as well. Blazing creatures of righteousness shining before the throne of God is an interpretation accepted by many.

and from Jesus Christ ... (v. 5)
The greetings are from "*him who is and who was, and who is to come*," from "*the seven spirits before his throne*," and "*from Jesus Christ*." Jesus is the Commander of Troops. He is our General, the "captain" of our salvation (Heb. 2:10, NKJV). The name "Jesus" is quite interesting. It is a Greek translation of the Hebrew word "Joshua," which means "God is my salvation." When the angel spoke to Joseph he told him that Mary was about to give birth to a son, and that he should "*give him the name Jesus, because he will save his people from their sins*" (Matt. 1:21). Jesus' name describes His mission. The Captain of our salvation came to bring us victory over sin.

The word "Christ" is a Greek translation of the Hebrew word "Messiah," which means "one who is anointed." The descriptions of Jesus given in this verse – "*the faithful witness, the firstborn from the dead, and the ruler of the kings of the earth*" – are very messianic. In the Old Testament, there are three anointed positions: prophet, priest, and king. A prophet brings the word of God to the nation. Elisha, for example, is anointed as a prophet prior to beginning his ministry (1 Kings 19:16). A priest offers sacrifices to God. Aaron and his sons are anointed in order to minister as priests before the Lord (Exod. 28:41). Kings, also, are anointed with oil prior to inauguration (n. 1 Sam. 16:13). These three powerful Old Testament offices are a shadow of the reality to come. When early Christians referred to Jesus as the Christ (n. Matt. 16:16; John 4:24-25), they announced to the world that they had found the One able to unite all three offices and bring victory to the people of God.

Jesus is the Anointed Prophet. Christians believe He is the One promised by Moses (Deut. 18:15); He is the Word of God who became flesh (John 1:1, 14). The term *"faithful witness"* refers to Christ's prophetic role. A witness in a court of law is one who tells the truth about something he or she has seen. Jesus came to bear witness to the truths of God. He is also the Anointed Priest. Christians believe He is a *"priest forever, in the order of Melchizedek"* (Heb. 7:17; cf. Ps. 110:4; Gen. 14:18-20), who *"appeared once for all at the end of the ages to do away with sin by the sacrifice of himself"* (Heb. 9:26). The expression *"firstborn from the dead"* captures Christ's priestly role, referencing the sacrifice He made on the cross, as well as His subsequent resurrection. He is the first to rise from the dead, and will be joined in resurrection by all who follow Him. Finally, Jesus is the Anointed King. He is the *"King of kings and the Lord of lords"* (Rev. 19:16). Before Him, every knee bows, and every tongue confesses that He is Lord (Phil. 2:10-11). The expression *"ruler of the kings of the earth"* captures the kingly aspect of our Messiah.

To him who ... has freed us from our sins by his blood ... (v. 5)
As John reflects upon the greetings extended to us by the great God of heaven, he offers praise. This God loves us, and has *"freed us from our sins by his blood."* A soldier who throws himself on a grenade, saving those around him from death, is the image that comes to mind. This is the price God has paid to secure our freedom. He gave His Son in order that we might live. *"It was not with perishable things such as silver or gold that you were redeemed from the empty way of life handed down to you ... but with the precious blood of Christ"* (1 Pet. 1:18-19; cf. Mark. 10:45; 1 Cor. 6:20). Does not this inspire you to continue, "fighting the good fight" for which Christ gave His life? Does not this encourage you to invite others to join in? Out of gratitude for what this great Warrior has done, we should follow.

To him who ... has made us to be a kingdom and priests ... (v. 6)
The praise continues. These words are in the past tense; they refer to John and to all who believe. In addition to saving our lives, the great General has equipped us with everything we need for battle. He has taken us from our sorry, sinful circumstances and has clothed us with the glory enjoyed originally in the Garden of Eden. He has made us kings and priests, officers and chiefs in His Army. We wear our uniforms with pride; everything we do is in the name of the Command, reflecting the character of the God we serve. The manner in which we live our lives should inspire others to follow.

In the Old Testament the nation of Israel was referred to as *"a kingdom of priests and a holy nation"* (Exod. 19:6), but New Testament writers apply the phrase to the Church, made up of people from all nations of the world (1 Pet. 2:9). The Book of Revelation refers to believers in this manner on two other occasions (5:10; 20:6).

Look, he is coming with the clouds ... (v. 7)
One of the abiding images of WWII was the promise made by General Douglas MacArthur to the people of the Philippines. When the Japanese Imperial Army drove MacArthur and the Allied armies from the shores of the besieged nation in 1942, his promise "I shall return" filled the Filipino people with great hope. It inspired them to join the resistance, and not compromise with the occupiers of their land.

On a much more significant level, John reminds us of Jesus' promise to return. He reiterated the vision of the prophet Daniel who saw *"one like a son of man, coming with the clouds of heaven"* (Dan. 7:13). Jesus told His disciples that His coming would be sudden (Matt. 24:27), and that He would return *"on the clouds of the sky, with power and great glory"* (Matt. 24:30; cf. Matt. 26:64). His return would bring about the destruction of the "lawless one" (2 Thess. 2:8), and set up a new heaven and new earth (2 Pet. 3:13). We are to be patient (James. 5:7) as we await His coming, disregarding the comments of scoffers who say *"Where is this 'coming' he promised?"* (2 Pet. 3:4).

Four times in the Book of Revelation, Jesus spoke the words "*I am coming soon*" (3:11; 22:7, 12, 20). These words constitute the hope of the Church; they bring comfort to those who struggle with injustice, and assist recruiters in signing up spiritual warriors for the Army of God.

every eye will see him, even those who pierced him ... (v. 7)
MacArthur's return was quite visible. Photographs of the general wading ashore are among the most famous images captured on film during WWII. The defeat of the Allied armies was now reversed. The Japanese oppressors were soon to be driven from the Philippine Islands.

This verse is an obvious reference to the crucifixion (cf. Zech. 12:10). The Great General of the Heavenly Armies was put to death on a cross, but the defeat was reversed – first by the resurrection, and eventually by His return. And there will be no doubt when He comes back: "*Every eye will see him.*" The Second Coming of our

General will not take place in secret, visible only to a select few. It will be very public, and when it happens, those who oppress the earth will be driven from it.

I am the Alpha and the Omega ... the Almighty ... (v. 8)
Jesus uses the first and last letters of the Greek alphabet to conclude His greetings to those who show up at the recruiting office. The letters symbolize eternity. Jesus has no beginning; He knows no end, and His power is limitless. Those who join His Army tap into unlimited resources.

your brother and companion ... (v. 9)
The lead recruiter for the Lord's Army now shares his own personal testimony. John is *our* brother and companion. It is so liberating to realize that the men and women of the Bible were ordinary human beings. If the author of Revelation was John the Apostle, he was originally a fisherman whose life was changed by Jesus Christ. He is our companion *"in the suffering and kingdom and patient endurance that are ours in Jesus."*

in the suffering ... (v. 9)
John suffered much for his faith. If this is the Apostle, he was imprisoned on numerous occasions (Acts 4:3; 5:18). This verse tells us he was on the island of Patmos because of his testimony for Christ.

Those who sign up in God's Army will experience much suffering. The good recruiter will never suggest that all one has to do is "accept Jesus in his or her heart, and everything will be all right." We do not wish to bring people into this Army under false pretenses. There will be great trials as you serve the Lord. Many of God's greatest warriors face terrible times of persecution. Joseph (Gen. 39:20), Elijah (1 Kings 19:2), Jeremiah (Jer. 38:6), Daniel (Dan. 6:16), David (Ps. 119:157), John the Baptist (Mark 6:17), Stephen (Acts 8:1), Paul (2 Cor. 11:23-33), and all of the Apostles (Acts 5:41) suffer enormously as they serve in the Army of the Most High. It is false teaching to suggest to a potential recruit that those who walk with Christ will not suffer. It is a lie to hint that all afflictions will be taken away if one prays and has enough faith (n. Mark 14:36; 2 Cor. 12:7-10).

Jesus taught his followers that there will be people who *"will lay hands on you and persecute you ... You will be betrayed even by parents, brothers, relatives and friends, and they will put some of you to death. All men will hate you because of me"* (Luke 21:12,16-17; cf. Ps. 116:15). He also said, *"Rejoice and be glad ... for in the same way they persecuted the prophets who were before you"* (Matt. 5:12). (Often, these are the feelings military recruiters experience as they attempt to make quota.)

Peter's first letter to the Church deals entirely with the subject of suffering. For a concluding thought, he wrote: *"And the God of all grace, who called you to his eternal glory in Christ, after you have suffered a little while, will himself restore you and make you strong"* (1 Pet. 5:10).

The Apostle Paul taught the early Christians in Rome that if *"we share in his sufferings ... we may also share in his glory"* (Rom. 8:17). To the church in Philippi he said: *"For it has been granted to you on behalf of Christ not only to believe on him, but also to suffer for him"* (Phil. 1:29). To the young man Timothy he declared, *"If we suffer, we shall also reign with him"* (2 Tim. 2:12, KJV). Therefore, with Paul, we would conclude: *"Endure hardship with us like a good soldier of Christ Jesus"* (2 Tim. 2:3).

and kingdom ... (v. 9)
John is also our companion in the kingdom. We do not needlessly suffer, because our ultimate goal is the kingdom of God. The kingdoms of this world operate by violence, subterfuge and fear; and much of the Book of Revelation deals with their demise. The kingdom of God, however, does not operate in this manner. His kingdom is *"righteousness, peace and joy"* (Rom. 14:17); it is not a political kingdom, but a spiritual reality (Acts 1:6-8). The kingdom of God is never propagated by war or violence (John 18:36), yet it breaks into our world and into our lives. Its growth is unstoppable. People

often ask: "Why do bad things happen?" A better question might be: "Why does anything good happen?" The answer is because God's Army is making an impact in our world, offering a kingdom that will endure forever.

The message of the kingdom of God is the primary thrust of the New Testament. John the Baptist preached that, *"the kingdom of heaven is near"* (Matt. 3:2). Jesus went throughout Galilee *"preaching the good news of the kingdom"* (Matt. 4:23, cf. Matt. 4:17; 9:35; Mark 1:15; Acts 1:3). He told Nicodemus: *"No one can see the kingdom of God unless he is born again"* (John 3:3). He told the Apostles to preach about the kingdom of God (Matt. 10:7; Luke 9:2), and it was the focus of both Philip's (Acts 8:12) and Paul's ministries (Acts 19:8; 20:25; 28:23, 31). As recruiters, we join with John and invite others to participate in this glorious kingdom.

and patient endurance ... (v. 9)
As "kingdom" people, we have already experienced much blessing from God, but we long for that blessing to come in its fullness. We are weary of evil and of oppressive situations, but as soldiers we must be patient. In much of Scripture we see a longing for the "not yet" part of the kingdom. The Psalmist cries out, *"My soul thirsts for God, for the living God. When can I go and meet with God?"* (Ps. 42:2). Paul writes: *"we ourselves, who have the firstfruits of the Spirit, groan inwardly as we wait eagerly for our adoption as sons, the redemption of our bodies"* (Rom. 8:23). John is our companion as we await the outworking of God's plans.

On the Lord's Day I was in the Spirit ... (v. 10)
Although Christians often call Sunday the "Lord's Day," nothing in Scripture makes this connection. The above text most likely refers to the end of the world. John, on the island of Patmos, was given a vision of the great Day of the Lord – a day when *"the LORD Almighty is mustering an army for war ... a cruel day, with wrath and fierce anger,"* a day when He will *"make the land desolate and destroy the sinners within it"* (Isa. 13:4, 9). John is a seasoned veteran;

he knows what is involved in spiritual warfare, and has been given a glimpse of the final battle plans. He is preeminently qualified to recruit others for service.

A loud voice like a trumpet ... (v. 10)
It was the sound of a trumpet that awakened John from his reverie. Modern armies still use the trumpet to sound attention, reveille, or taps. In the Scriptures, the trumpet was often sounded to announce Divine activity. A trumpet summoned Moses to the top of Mt. Sinai (Exod. 19:16). Trumpets were used *"for calling the community together and for having the camps set out"* (Num. 10:2), for declaring war (Num. 10:9), and for announcing appointed feasts and festivals (Num. 10:10). Trumpets triggered the collapse of the walls in Jericho (Josh. 6:20), were sounded upon the coronation of kings (1 Kings 1:34; 2 Kings 9:13), and used to warn people of impending disaster (Jer. 4:5).

Write on a scroll ... (v. 11)
There is always an enormous amount of administration that accompanies military operations. (It is often said that the Navy floats on paperwork.) Deck logs are meticulously maintained on every warship.

John was to write down the events of the war that unfolded before his eyes. He may have used a scroll made of papyrus or a carefully prepared animal skin known as parchment.[25] Occasionally, parchment scrolls had writing on both sides. The scroll in Revelation chapter five was of this type (5:1; cf. Exod. 32:15; Ezek. 2:10).

I saw seven golden lampstands ... (v. 12)
When John turned to see the voice that was speaking to him, he saw seven golden lampstands. These were the seven churches (n. 1:20) to whom he would send his epistle. Lamps are to bring light; they are to shine in the darkness. The seven-branch lampstands, mounted in front of the Holy of Holies, illuminated the ancient tabernacle of the Israelites (Exod. 25:31-37; Lev. 24:4), as well as Solomon's temple (1 Kings 7:49). The Church in our era is to bring the light of Christ into the darkness of the world.

Jesus referred to Himself as *"the light of the world"* (John 8:12). In the Sermon on the Mount, He said the same thing to those who follow Him (Matt. 5:14). Our General came to cast out the darkness, and we who serve in His Army are called to do the same. *"Let your light shine before men, that they may see your good deeds and praise your Father in heaven"* (Matt. 5:16).

Recruiting is only part of the Church's comprehensive "warfighting effort." In addition, She serves on the front lines of spiritual warfare, standing up to the sea beast and the earth beast,[26] challenging the enemy's occupation of territory that belongs to God.

---

[25]Interestingly enough, Pergamum, one of the cities to whom the Book of Revelation was addressed, was a great center of the writing material industry. Our word "parchment" is a derivative of the Greek word "Pergamum."

[26]See chapter six for a discussion of these enemy combatants.

Similar to a battalion in the army, or to a ship of the line in the navy, the local church is on the "tip of the spear" when it comes to advancing the kingdom of God. The spiritual weapons it employs throw the enemy off balance, casting out areas of darkness by allowing the light of Christ to shine forth. Those who are recruited into the Lord's Army must participate in the local church. There are no one man fighting holes; that would soon lead to despair. A soldier cannot go to war all by himself; he or she must be affiliated with a unit. There are no lone rangers in God's Army; we are in this together.

among the lampstands was someone "like a son of man" ... (v. 13)
The expression "son of man" points us to the prophet Daniel, who saw the kingdoms of this world rise and fall before his eyes. At the end of the age, only one kingdom was left standing. The "son of man" was its king:

> *"In my vision at night I looked, and there before me was one like a son of man, coming with the clouds of heaven. He approached the Ancient of Days and was led into his presence. He was given authority, glory and sovereign power; all peoples, nations and men of every language worshiped him. His dominion is an everlasting dominion that will not pass away, and his kingdom is one that will never be destroyed"* (Dan. 7:13-14).

Throughout the Gospels Jesus Christ refers to himself as the "son of man" (Matt. 10:23; 13:41; 24:27). In the same way as the general of an army or the admiral of a fleet stands among the soldiers or sailors, especially during very significant moments, here Jesus stands in the midst of our churches. This can be very inspirational for the troops, especially as they are about to enter into battle.

dressed in a robe ... and with a golden sash ... (vv. 13-15)
The full dress uniforms of an admiral or a general are breathtaking. They are meant to inspire awe and respect. In this text, the garments of Jesus were similar to those of the Old Testament high

priest (n. Exod. 28:4; 29:8; 39:29), but far more glorious. Standing before John was the great High Priest who had *"gone through the heavens"* (Heb. 4:14). If the author was the Apostle, he may have seen the glorified Jesus on an earlier occasion at the Mount of Transfiguration (Matt. 17:1-6; cf. Acts 9:4-5). The white hair of the Heavenly Judge is also mentioned in Daniel's prophecy (Dan. 7:9), and it speaks of honor (Prov. 16:31). British judges even to the present day don white wigs in a courtroom of law. As John saw the eyes of Christ blazing like fire, his feet glowing like bronze, and a double-edged sword coming out of His mouth (cf. Heb. 4:12-13; Rev. 19:15), he was prepared to listen.

he held seven stars ... (v. 16)
"The seven stars are the angels of the seven churches" (1:20). The Greek word for "angel" can also be translated as "messenger." This prompts many to suggest that Revelation was written to the pastors of the seven churches. Each of the seven letters begins with *"To the angel of the church in..."* (2:1, 8, 12, 18; 3:1, 7, 14). Pastors, certainly, are among the unsung heroes of our era. Often, there is no glamour, little recognition, and meager pay for their work, yet they are on the front lines of battle, leading the people of God in spiritual warfare.

Others believe that actual angels, warriors in God's Heavenly Army, are being addressed. The Bible indicates that guardian angels may watch over the affairs of humanity. The appearances of angels to Daniel (Dan. 10), and to Peter (Acts 12), and the words of Jesus to His disciples, *"Do not look down on one of these little ones. For I tell you that their angels in heaven always see the face of my Father in heaven,"* (Matt. 18:10) are of particular interest. If these words do address angels, the ultimate readers remain the people of God, and both come under the authority of Him who walks among the lampstands.

I fell at his feet as though dead ... (v. 17)
John had come face to face with the true and the living God. Surely, this must have instilled a passion for recruiting! We want to make sure we are serving this great Warrior, not taking a stance against Him. When Moses requested to see God, the LORD answered, *"you cannot see my face, for no one may see me and live"* (Exod. 33:20).   When Isaiah the prophet saw him, he cried out, *"Woe to me! ... I am ruined! For I am a man of unclean lips, and I live among a people of unclean lips"* (Isa. 6:5). Like John on Patmos, Joshua (5:14), Ezekiel (1:28), Daniel (10:9), and all of the disciples (Matt. 17:6; Acts 26:14) fell flat on their faces when they came into the presence of the Holy One. Let us not underestimate this. God is more than "the Good Man upstairs." He is the Lord God, the Creator of the heavens and the earth, and *"It is a fearful thing to fall into the hands of the living God"* (Heb. 10:31, KJV).

Do not be afraid ... (v. 17)
These were the first words that John heard after being restored to his senses. They may be the very first words that soldiers of the Most High will hear upon leaving this world for the next. The all-powerful God is also very merciful, and those who love Him will experience this mercy. In every one of the encounters mentioned above, God came with a hand of grace to take away the fear. An angel spoke to Isaiah and said, *"your guilt is taken away and your sin atoned for"* (Isa. 6:7). To Ezekiel, the Lord said, *"Son of man, stand up on your feet and I will speak to you"* (Ezek. 2:1). A hand reached out, touched Daniel, and set him on his hands and knees (Dan. 10:10). On the Mount of Transfiguration, Jesus came and touched His disciples. *"Get up,"* He told them, *"Don't be afraid"* (Matt. 17:7).

In C.S. Lewis' seven-part children's series entitled *The Chronicles of Narnia*, there is a lion by the name of Aslan who is lord of Narnia. According to Lewis,

> People who have not been in Narnia sometimes think that a thing cannot be good and terrible at the same time. If the children had ever thought so, they were cured of it now. For when they tried to look at Aslan's face they just caught a glimpse of the golden mane and the great, royal, solemn, overwhelming eyes; and then they found they couldn't look at him and went all trembly.[27]

A truly great military leader cares for the men and women who serve under him. The great God of all heaven and earth, whose appearances strike such fear in the hearts of frail human beings, loves us.

Throughout Scripture, as the people of God step out in faith, they are exhorted to "not be afraid." This was the message God gave to Abram when he was asked to leave the land of Ur (Gen. 15:1), as well as His word to Hagar as she consoled her son (Gen. 21:17). God told Moses and the Israelites, *"Do not be afraid,"* as they left the land of Egypt (Exod. 14:13), and again as they entered the land of Canaan (Deut. 1:21). In the New Testament, as the world prepared for the arrival of God's Son, angelic visits to Joseph (Matt. 1:20), Zechariah (Luke 1:13), Mary (Luke 1:30) and the shepherds (Luke 2:10) were accompanied by these words. The women who came to the tomb on Easter Sunday were told, *"Do not be afraid"* (Matt. 28:5).

These are God's words to His people as they lie in hospital beds, or awake at night worrying about the future. These are God's words to us, as we step out in faith, struggling against the dragon, the sea beast and the earth beast. As we read the Book of Revelation, it is God who is waging war against these powers. The fierce judgments that are coming upon the earth are directed against those who resist His will. Those who follow Christ have nothing to fear.

---

[27] C.S. Lewis, *The Lion, the Witch, and the Wardrobe*, (New York: Collier Books, 1974), 123.

I am the Living One … (v. 18)
In rising from the dead, Jesus emerged victorious from the greatest of all battles. He overcame death itself – *"Death has been swallowed up in victory"* (1 Cor. 15:54). In following Him, we too shall have life to its fullest. The enemy will have no power over us. Through John, the great General of the Armies makes the same statement and poses the same question to the potential recruit as He did to Martha long ago: *"Whoever lives and believes in me will never die. Do you believe this?"* (John 11:25).

I hold the keys of death and Hades … (v. 18)
Death, the grave, the Greek word "Hades", and the Hebrew word "Sheol," are synonyms. Prior to the coming of Christ, what happened after death was a great mystery. Although there are still many unanswered questions about what happens when we leave this world, it is no longer completely unknown. Christ shattered the power of death, and opened up the gates of Hades. *"Listen,"* the Apostle Paul writes, *"I tell you a mystery: We will not all sleep … the dead will be raised imperishable"* (1 Cor. 15:51-52). Most of us fear death more than anything else, but it is an enemy that our General has overcome. When the potential recruit decides to trust the leadership of our Commander, he or she is promised victory over this nemesis.

Write, therefore, what you have seen … (vv. 19-20)
The Commanding General has given the lead recruiter a command to write down the things that he has been privileged to see. As we noted in the introduction, some of the things that John sees have already taken place – *"what is now"* – while some of them have not yet happened – *"what will take place later."* The vision given to John is to be written down and sent to the seven "angels" of the seven churches.

Summary of Revelation chapter one
As we conclude chapter one of the Book of Revelation, we have been introduced to the Commander of troops who has extended personal greetings. We have also become acquainted with John, a seasoned veteran in spiritual warfare, chief among the Lord's recruiters, and author of the text. John was given special insight into the war that Jesus Christ is leading. While in the recruiting office, we have learned about the benefits of joining this mighty Army, but we are also sobered by what will happen to those who oppose it. Those who enlist will be assigned to local churches and have a responsibility to serve in them. In the next chapter, the letter that John sent to each of the seven churches serves as a training manual, transforming "civilians" into spiritual warriors. In essence, what takes place is spiritual boot camp for those who agree to serve in the Lord's Army.

Chapter 2

BOOT CAMP

(Revelation 2:1-3:22)

When my son left home he had no motivation, he was lazy, slobby, no pride, no self worth ... The man that I met on Thursday for parents day is AWESOME ... He looks different, he walks different, he talks different, he has such a sense of bearing and pride all I could do was look at him in awe.[28]
  - "Cybil," Mother of a Marine

To the angel of the church in ... (2:1)
The Marine Corps Recruit Depot (MCRD) in San Diego, CA, graduates approximately 20,000 Marines every year. Recruits are assigned to one of twelve companies and undergo a rigorous twelve-week training regimen designed to "purge nasty civilian habits from their bodies," and transform them into hardened warriors.

Recruits show up to MCRD on buses. Upon arrival they are met by a drill instructor (the D.I.) who "urges" them to get off quickly and line up on the yellow footprints outside of the receiving company headquarters. Once roll call is taken, recruits get haircuts, receive medical and dental screenings, and are issued a basic uniform allowance. Shortly afterwards, each man (there are only men at MCRD San Diego) is assigned to a company, and the

---
[28]Available from http://4mermarine.com/usmc/quotes.html; Internet.

training begins. During the seventy training days, a daunting schedule of events is maintained. Recruits learn military history and terminology; they are taught teamwork, respect for self and for others, and the value of not quitting. Rigorous physical training, swimming qualifications, military drill, weapons handling and firing, and schooling in the martial arts takes place. At each point in the training, drill instructors look for strengths for which recruits are praised, and for weaknesses which require additional instruction.

At the end of the training period, those recruits who: 1) display honor, courage, and commitment; 2) make an honest attempt to accomplish all tasks; 3) exhibit discipline, teamwork, and *esprit de corps*; and 4) receive a favorable recommendation from the Senior Drill Instructor, are awarded the "Eagle, Globe, and Anchor," and may claim the title of "United States Marine." Marine Corps boot camp is intended to make the recruits successful, both in their military careers and in future civilian undertakings. Boot camp is not fun: it is very difficult, but once a young man or young woman has completed it, a genuine transformation has taken place, and warriors capable of defending their nation have been cultivated. As Marines will often tell you, "MCRD is not a good place to be at, but it is a good place to be from."

For those who are beginning their walk with Jesus, catechism class or periods of pre-baptismal instruction could be considered "spiritual boot camp." In such settings, candidates learn information about the great God they serve, and experience personal transformation as they grow in faith and obedience. One might consider John's letter to the seven churches as a training guide for those who have been recruited into the Army of the Most High. Each of the segments follows a very regimented format. Jesus, the great Warrior, commands John to write to "*the angel of the church in…*", while extending introductory greetings using imagery from chapter one. Following the introduction, He employs the expression "*I know your…*", in order to point out particular areas where the church is doing well. (And no one knows you better than the D.I. – both a frightening and a comforting thought.) A listing of problem areas, matters that hamper the witness of God's people and make for an ineffective "fighting force," follows the words of praise. Christ then suggests a course of action to remedy those problems. If the church fails to take remedial action, harsh consequences are to be expected. Each segment closes with a promise to the one "*who overcomes*," and with the cryptic words, "*He who has an ear, let him hear what the Spirit says to the churches.*"

The seven churches of Revelation (and they were addressed according to their location along the ancient trading route) struggled to bring the gospel of Jesus Christ to bear upon the culture of the ancient Roman Empire. There was (and is) a tendency for human government to arrogate powers that do not belong to it. (In chapter six we will closely analyze the sea beast, a symbol of human government gone wrong.) The State often claims for itself authority that belongs only to God. There is also a tendency for the Church to become so enamored with temporal politics that She loses Her prophetic witness. (This also will be discussed in chapter six, as we look at the machinations of the earth beast.) Much of what John writes to the seven churches is harsh. (And all of his words are read to each of the congregations.) The tone is accusatorial. The

Drill Instructor is "in your face." Ephesus had forsaken her first love (2:4); Christians there may have been more worried about what Caesar had to say than in obeying the commands of the General of the Heavenly Armies. Smyrna had to deal with *"the slander of those who say they are Jews and are not"* (2:9) – a reference, perhaps to some sort of "civil religion," where being a citizen of Rome was more important than being a citizen of the kingdom of God. "Satan" had his throne in Pergamum (2:13) – no doubt a veiled reference to the Imperial regime. Many there played the role of Balaam (2:14) and compromised their faith. Similar problems existed in each of the other worshipping communities.

As mentioned above, the term "seven churches" also serves as a symbol for the Church universal. In addition to addressing very specific issues in a fixed historical context, John's words ring true to every generation of believers. In much the same way as warriors from every age and nationality study such works as Sun Tzu's *The Art of War,* Clausewitz's *On War,* or Mahan's *The Influence of Sea Power upon History*, the Book of Revelation serves as a guide to educate spiritual warriors in every era, from every denomination. When Revelation was written, there were churches all over the Roman Empire that had the strengths and weaknesses of these seven. Throughout 2000 years of Church history, across national boundaries, and among bodies of believers today, this is still the case. The words made sense to the original recipients, they connected with believers throughout the Christian era, and they speak to us today. The words are written about us and to us. If we have ears to hear, we will benefit immensely from what the Spirit has to say.

Ephesus ... (2:1-7)
Some soldiers do all the right things, but they have no heart. With such, you would not want to go into battle. This was the problem in Ephesus. Although the church's theology may have been correct, there was no passion for service. In God's boot camp, the church was warned to repent, or the lampstand would be removed from its place (v. 5).[29]

---
[29]Interestingly enough, there is not even a city of Ephesus today. See Michael Wilcock, *I Saw Heaven Opened: The Message of Revelation* (Downers Grove, Illinois: InterVarsity Press, 1975), 44.

Ephesus was the largest of the seven cities, a well-established metropolis situated on a beautiful harbor at the crossroads of three major trade routes.[30] It could be thought of as the "New York City" of its day. Having a population of approximately 250,000, the city was proud of a stadium that could seat 25,000 spectators, and it had a huge, well-known market. Ephesus was best known for the temple constructed in honor of Diana (Artemis), the Greek goddess of fertility. Considered one of the seven wonders of the ancient world, it housed an army of prostitutes and eunuchs, and was the site of much drinking and rowdiness. The original temple, destroyed by fire in 356 BC, was four times the size of the majestic Parthenon, currently gracing Mars Hill in Athens. The ancient marvel was 425' long, 220' wide, 60' high, and was supported by 127 marble pillars. The temple was later rebuilt, but not quite to the scale of the original.[31]

John commended the church in Ephesus because it hated "*the practices of the Nicolaitans*" (v. 6). Although nobody knows much about this ancient heresy, it seems to have plagued the churches in Pergamum (2:15) and Thyatira (2:20-21) as well. When the Apostle Paul warned the Ephesian elders that "*savage wolves will come in among you and will not spare the flock*" (Acts 20:29), it may be that he had this group in mind. Mounce believes that the Nicolaitans may have "worked out a compromise with the pagan society in which they lived."[32] The Ephesian Christians were correct in going after the false teachings of this group, but they were doing it in the wrong spirit. It may be that as church leadership brought chastisement, the motivation was more about having the right theology than it was about loving one's neighbor. As Wilcock notes, there

---

[30]The Apostle Paul spent two years of his life in the city of Ephesus. Acts chapter nineteen describes much of the ministry that took place during his stay. The New Testament letter to the Ephesians is one that is noted for theological richness and practical application. The city may also have been the hometown of the Apostle John in his later years.
[31]Mounce, 85-86.
[32]Ibid., 89.

are often Christians who "cast themselves in the role of Mr. Valiant-for-Truth," but "have forgotten that they are also expected to be Mr. Great-heart."[33]

In reminding the church to *"Remember the height from which you have fallen! Repent and do the things you did at first"* (v. 5), John reinforced the need for believers to follow the great commands of our General – those of loving God and of loving one's neighbor (Mt. 22:34-40). He appealed to the church's collective memory, much in the same way that Jesus appealed to the memory of the wayward son. When the Prodigal found himself slopping hogs and eating the crusts that were left behind, he remembered that even his father's servants fared better. In much the same way, John was appealing to the church in Ephesus to return to her first love.

Smyrna ... (2:8-11)

Boot camp involves great trials. Recruits face intense physical and psychological pressures involving periods of hunger, sleep deprivation, and physical exhaustion. Drill instructors expect teamwork and problem solving during these difficult training periods, and more often than not, the trying situations bring out the very best in the young men and women who have signed up to serve their country. The church in Smyrna faced great trials, yet her faith and generosity served as an example to Christians everywhere.

Like Ephesus, Smyrna was a harbor town, best known for having been the birthplace of the poet Homer. By the time Revelation was written, the city had a population of about 200,000, a rather noteworthy fact considering that it had been completely destroyed seven hundred years earlier, and had lain in ruins for three centuries. Smyrna was a city that had "risen from the dead,"[34] so greetings from him who *"died and came to life again"* (v. 8) were particularly meaningful. A temple was built in Smyrna to honor Tiberius Caesar, and anyone who failed to confess his deity was likely to face fierce persecution. Of the seven cities to which letters were addressed, only Smyrna exists today.[35]

---

[33]Wilcock, 44.
[34]Ibid., 45.
[35]Mounce, 91.

Believers suffered for their faith, and many lost jobs because they refused to worship Caesar. The lack of employment soon led to poverty. Today there are churches that suggest, "if you give your life to Jesus, He will grant you material prosperity, good health and worldly blessing," but there are many more that can relate to the trials of the church in Smyrna. In the recent past, African-American congregations in the American South, and underground churches in the former Soviet Union understood what Christ meant when He said, "*I know your afflictions and your poverty – yet you are rich*" (v. 9). Churches in Communist China or under radical Islamic regimes can relate to these words as well.

The church in Smyrna was commended for its faith during times of trial, the worst of which may have come from false believers within the congregation. "*The slander of those who say they are Jews*" (v. 9) probably refers to men and women who publicly professed faith in God, but secretly cooperated with the Caesar-worshipping government for personal advancement, a manifestation of the earth beast (see chapter six). Betrayal or rejection by those closest to you is often the worst kind of pain. Jesus made note of this during His earthly ministry:

> "*If you were Abraham's children ... then you would do the things Abraham did. As it is, you are determined to kill me ... Abraham did not do such things ... you belong to your father, the devil*" (John 8:39-40, 44; cf. Acts 6:8-9; 14:19).

God exhorted the church to "*not be afraid of what you are about to suffer ... even to the point of death*" (v. 10). Polycarp, the bishop of Smyrna, was martyred for his faith only a few years after these words were written. In the midst of an ongoing persecution he was asked to renounce his faith in Jesus Christ or lose his life. The elderly man chose the latter, and his words were recorded for posterity. "For eighty-six years I have been his servant, and he has done me no wrong. How can I blaspheme my King who saved me?"[36]

---

[36]*The Apostolic Fathers: Second Edition,* ed. Michael W. Holmes, trans. J.B. Lightfoot and J.R. Harmer (Grand Rapids, Michigan: Baker Book House, 1989), 139.

There are consequences to placing one's faith in Christ. In today's military (or in American society at large), the fear of ridicule from one's peers often causes soldiers, otherwise men and women of great courage, to deny or hide their faith. In many nations, the cost of believing in Jesus is far more substantial than the petty persecutions we face.[37] God encouraged the faithful in Smyrna, as He encourages us, to live their lives with integrity, regardless of the consequences. To suffer persecution for one's faith is not unlike the sacrifices a soldier might make on a battlefield. And if our stance were to result in death, that would not be the end, for we have the additional promise of resurrection. Our General has said, "*Do not be afraid of those who kill the body but cannot kill the soul. Rather, be afraid of the One who can destroy both soul and body in hell*" (Mt. 10:28). Persecution is a given; there will be a certain amount of suffering that will accompany your faith. The expression, "*you will suffer persecution for ten days*" (v. 10), should be read symbolically, ten being a number that suggests "thorough, complete, and ongoing" (cf. Gen. 31:7; Nu. 14:22; Job 19:3).

Spiritual warriors who do not compromise with the powers of this world bring strength to the Church and credibility to its message. As the Church father Tertullian once wrote, "The blood of the martyrs is the seed of the Church."[38] Christ's ultimate message to Smyrna and to us is: "Fear not, our God is bigger than the gods of this world." Death, our final enemy, has been defeated. "*The crown of life*" (v. 10) will be given to those who remain faithful.[39]

---

[37] According to Everett Ferguson, "Did You Know," and James Reapsome, "Persecuted Christians Today," *Christian History* 9, no. 3 (1990): inside front cover, 37, "more people have been martyred for Christ in the past fifty years than in the church's first three hundred years." This would include horrible persecutions against believers in the former Soviet Union (where perhaps over 30 million believers died for their faith), in communist China (where, during the Cultural Revolution of 1966-76, religious activity was forced underground, most Bibles were destroyed, and believers were imprisoned or executed), and in Uganda (where approximately 400,000 Christians died, disappeared, or fled the country between 1971 and 1976).

[38] Tertullian, *Apologeticus,* 17.

[39] Warren W. Wiersbe, *Be Victorious* (Wheaton, Illinois: Victor Books, 1985), 29, suggests that this imagery is highly appropriate for the city of Smyrna, a place where annual athletic games were held, and crowns were awarded to the victors.

Pergamum ... (2:12-17)
Marine recruits are taught to "accomplish the mission at hand," and to "take care of your fellow Marine." Sailors are taught "one hand for the man, one hand for the ship." In taking care of their own, Marine warriors must be doctrinally sound. They must have an understanding of tactics and strategy, and know how and when to use their weapons. Ignorance will endanger others. Sailors must be intimately familiar with their ships and how they operate. If a ship sinks due to incompetence, all on board will perish, rendering such platitudes as "looking out for each other" meaningless. In like manner, Christian warriors are commanded to love one another, but they are also responsible for certain truths expressed in the gospel, without which proclamations of love are made meaningless. To be incompetent or apathetic toward basic Christian teachings will endanger the eternal souls of others. The church in Pergamum was rebuked for these reasons.

Pergamum was an inland city, built on a cone-shaped hill, a thousand feet in height. One of its major industries was that of preparing parchments and papyrus scrolls for the writing of books. The city had a library containing 200,000 volumes, rivaling in size the library of ancient Alexandria. At the top of the hill stood the great altar of Zeus where several of the pagan gods were worshiped. In 29 BC, the Emperor Augustus granted permission that a temple be erected to "the divine Augustus and the goddess Roma," making this the first city in the Empire to build a temple dedicated to the worship of a living emperor.[40] The expression *"where Satan has his throne"* (v. 13) is undoubtedly a reference to this temple.[41]

The church in Pergamum was commended for remaining true to the name of the Lord Jesus Christ. Christians there did not renounce their faith even when the man Antipas (v. 13) was put to death. (We know nothing about this man.) But the church was rebuked because its leadership had set up "stumbling blocks" by

---
[40] Mounce, 95-96.
[41] Martin Rist, *The Modern Reader's Guide to the Book of Revelation* (New York: Association Press, 1961), 44.

tolerating false teaching. Unlike the church in Ephesus, many of the believers in Pergamum held *"to the teachings of the Nicolaitans"* (v. 15).[42]

Others adhered *"to the teaching of Balaam"* who enticed *"the Israelites to sin by eating food sacrificed to idols and by committing sexual immorality"* (v. 14). In the Old Testament, Balaam taught the Israelite men that it was okay to engage in relations with the Midianite women, even though the Law of God did not permit it (Num. 31:16; 25:1-2). Jude 11 suggests that he may have done this for financial gain (cf. Num. 22:7, 17-18, 37; 24:11-13). John's use of these expressions probably served as a veiled reference to those who would compromise with the oppressions of the Roman Empire rather than stand up against them.

The church in Pergamum was commanded to repent (v. 16). Leaders were to stand up against false doctrine and teach the truth. John was warning the church not to embrace everything that came out of Rome as "gospel." The image of the *"sharp, double-edged sword"* (v. 12) in his greeting served as a reminder of the power of God's Word (n. Heb. 4:12-13). In our day, church pastors are often financially dependent upon the congregations they lead. There are often great temptations to compromise, but the very Scriptures with which we have been entrusted remind us to hold firm to the things we have been taught (2 Thess. 2:15), not to be conformed *"to the pattern of this world"* (Rom. 12:2), and not to lay stumbling blocks before our brothers and sisters (1 Cor. 8:9-13). Many churches, so worried about offending people, avoid taking strong stances for the kingdom of God. As a result, the servants of God remain in an infantile state, needing milk, unable to digest solid food (Heb. 5:12). If foot soldiers in the local church take care of both "man and mission," God's kingdom will continue to advance.

---

[42]The problem in Pergamum was the opposite of that encountered by the church in Ephesus. The Ephesians strongly rebuked the heretical Nicolaitans, but they lacked love and compassion. The church in Pergamum lovingly accepted the Nicolaitans, but failed to reject their doctrines.

Thyatira ... (2:18-29)

Frequently, "booze, broads, or bucks" (to use a rather crass expression) lead to the moral downfall of many soldiers or sailors. The youngest of troops tend to get tangled up in alcohol or drug abuse in their attempts to escape the harsh realities of their training. Illicit affairs (regardless of gender) seem to afflict those who have become a little more established in their careers, while financial improprieties seem to be the bane of those who are more senior in rank. Nothing is more embarrassing to the military or to the nation than moral failure. Countless careers have been ruined and reputations soiled. When we become like the enemy, all of our efforts for good are in vain. The church in Thyatira lacked the moral authority to impact the world with the gospel of Jesus Christ because many of the believers did not "walk the talk."

Thyatira was an inland city, founded initially as a military outpost. It later became a center for manufacturing and marketing, and was noted especially for a large number of flourishing trade guilds. Lydia, a seller of purple cloth (Acts 16:14), came from Thyatira. The "divine guardian" of the city was the Greek sun-god Apollo, who was considered to be the "patron of the guilds," and was honored in any religious celebration.[43] Greetings to the church from the One who created the sun, *"whose eyes are like blazing fire"* (v. 18), were certainly appropriate.

John commends the church for its deeds, love, and perseverance, but rebukes it for moral failure. The problems that faced the church in Thyatira seem similar to those in Pergamum – *"sexual immorality and the eating of food sacrificed to idols"* (v. 20)[44] – but there was a major difference. In Pergamum, leaders of the church failed because they did not *speak out* against Christians who were compromising their faith. In Thyatira, the leadership was actually doing the compromising; John refers to one of them as *"that woman Jezebel who calls herself a prophetess"* (v. 20).

---

[43] Mounce, 101.
[44] This expression was likely a code, referring to those who would compromise with the Caesar-worshiping Imperium.

The reference was to the Old Testament Queen who lived her life in a highly immoral fashion. She married the king of Israel (1 Kings 16:31), but killed the prophets of the Lord (1 Kings 18:13), and ordered the death of many innocent people. The account of her stealing the vineyard of Naboth the Jezreelite (1 Kings 21:1-29) is particularly revolting. The strong words of judgment, "*I will make those who commit adultery with her suffer intensely,*" and "*I will strike her children dead*" (vv. 22-23), recall the gruesome death of this evil queen (2 Kings 9:30-37). The "Jezebel" of Thyatira was given numerous opportunities to repent, but she continued to teach and mislead the people of God.

Churches should select people for leadership positions based on moral considerations, as well as on their ability to lead. While wealth or social status may contribute to the selection process, great attention should be paid to proclivities such as racial prejudice, greed, gossip, or inappropriate sexual behavior. Such sin among leaders will quickly destroy the witness of an entire body of believers. When the sin is lived out in blatant rebellion, or taught to be acceptable behavior, its stench is particularly odious. Our Commanding General once said,

> *Things that cause people to sin are bound to come, but woe to that person through whom they come. It would be better for him to be thrown into the sea with a millstone tied around his neck than for him to cause one of these little ones to sin. So watch yourselves* (Luke 17:1-2).

Sardis ... (3:1-6)
In boot camp, recruits spend a significant amount of their time standing watch. This occurs all hours of the day and night, often under very trying circumstances. Recruits learn that falling asleep on watch is an offense punishable by Courts-Martial. In wartime, it can result in the death penalty. Vigilance is the price that must be paid to ensure freedom. The church in Sardis, although it had a good reputation, had fallen asleep.

Sardis was located fifty miles east of Ephesus on a mountain that towered 1500 feet over a broad fertile plain, making it nearly inaccessible to invading troops from any direction. The city was the capital of the ancient kingdom of Lydia, and was the first place in the world where gold and silver coins were minted. In addition, the art of dyeing wool may have been first introduced here. Despite obvious topographical advantages, Sardis was invaded twice during its long history, and on both occasions it was due to a lack of vigilance. In 549 BC, Cyrus the Great captured the city by "deploying a climber to work his way up a crevice on one of the nearly perpendicular walls of the mountain fortress." Later in the third century BC, the same thing happened. The gates to the city were opened from within, and enemy armies were able to enter. By the time the Book of Revelation was written, Sardis had lost much of its influence in the affairs of the world.[45]

The church in Sardis seems to have followed the same sociological pattern. It had a *"reputation of being alive"*, but was *"dead"* (v. 1). The slumbering body of believers was commanded to *"wake up!"* and *"strengthen what remains"* (v. 2). Christ warned the church that He would *"come like a thief"* (v. 3; cf. Matt. 24:42-43; 1 Thess. 5:2; 2 Pet. 3:10), that His coming would be sudden, and that there would be no time for repentance. There were, however, a few people in the city who had not *"soiled their clothes"* (v. 4), a reference, no doubt, to those who had not compromised their faith in order to win Caesar's approval. The church was warned to *"keep watch, because you do not know the day or the hour"* (Matt. 25:13).

There are many churches today that are rich in history and tradition. They have a good reputation, but there is no longer any power coming from the pulpit. The things which created a good reputation in the past are no longer being preached. Making people feel good has become more important than proclaiming the words

---

[45]Mounce, 108-111 passim.

of life.[46] This earth beast (see chapter six) is to be resisted. Perhaps you have worshipped at Sardis. You first visited because you heard good things about it, but soon departed because there was no spiritual life. Worshippers went through all the right motions during tradition-steeped rituals, but without enthusiasm or feeling. The music was antiquated, the sermons boring, and there was no relevance to the prevailing culture. People attended because of the church's reputation, and because it was "the proper thing to do."

Military personnel cannot rely on the valor displayed by heroes in by-gone eras. We must learn from those who have gone before us, but must also continually build upon the foundations they laid. The same is true in spiritual warfare. Christ offered hope to believers in Sardis by stating that they must *"Remember"* the things they *"have received and heard; obey... and repent"* (v. 3). This is one of the main reasons our Commander runs a boot camp.

Philadelphia ... (3:7-13)

Recruits in boot camp learn to accomplish assigned tasks, often with limited resources at their disposal. Upon hitting the fleet, graduates will discover that, as one recent Secretary of Defense stated, "We don't always go to war with the army we want, but with the army we have." On occasion, units have not had sufficient ammunition to accomplish needed training. Reservists have been known to purchase their own body armor prior to deploying, while junior enlisted families frequently require food stamps to make ends meet. The most successful of these warriors will voice concern about such conditions, but learn, if necessary, to "do more with less." The church in Philadelphia, apparently, had little influ-

---

[46]H. Richard Niebuhr, *Christ and Culture* (New York: Harper & Row, Publishers, Incorporated, 1951), 83-115, devotes an entire chapter to "The Christ of Culture." On p. 83 he writes, "In every culture to which the Gospel comes there are men who hail Jesus as the Messiah of their society ... they feel no great tension between the church and the world." This seems to be the type of Christianity found in Sardis. The great problem was, however, that in Sardis there should be have been great tension between Christ and the prevailing culture. Caesar was being worshipped as God, and the Church was accepting it. Christians there needed to "Wake up!"

ence on the surrounding culture; its message was "marginalized" by the powers that be, but its members had remained faithful to the gospel of Jesus Christ.

Philadelphia was an inland city, located at the juncture of several major trade routes. Its name in Greek means "brotherly love," and its founding in 189 BC reflected the love that a man by the name of Attalus showed his brother. Philadelphia was known as the "gateway to the East," and the city was one of great commercial importance. A volcanic plain lying to the north was very fertile and "well suited to growing grapes." Its strong economy, based on agriculture and industry, led to considerable prosperity. In AD 17, the city of Philadelphia was completely destroyed by a devastating earthquake. With help from the Roman Emperor, it was rebuilt and later renamed "Neocaesarea."[47]

The church in Philadelphia was commended for its perseverance, for keeping God's word, and for not denying His name. Believers faced internal pressures, similar to those faced by the church in Smyrna, coming from *"those who are of the synagogue of Satan, who claim to be Jews ... but are liars"* (v. 9; cf. Rev. 2:9). The Philadelphians were encouraged to *"Hold on"* (v. 11), because Jesus Christ is coming soon, and He will *"keep you from the hour of trial that is going to come upon the whole world"* (v. 10). The expression "hour of trial" is a symbolic reference to the "Day of the Lord," the final apocalyptic battle, where God will destroy all the forces of evil.[48] Jesus Christ will do the fighting. He *"holds the key of David"* (v. 7; cf. Isa. 22:22; 2 Sam. 7:12-13; Matt. 1:1), and will open a door

---

[47]Mounce, 114-115.

[48]Many Christians believe that the "hour of trial" refers to a future period of turmoil that will last for seven years. The last three and one half years of this time period will be known as the "Great Tribulation." This text is then "proof" that the Church will not go through the Great Tribulation. Although the expression "great tribulation" is used twice in the Book of Revelation (2:22, KJV; 7:14), and several other places in Scripture, nowhere is it defined as a period of three and one half years. This is an interpretation that is read into the text. Christ's word to the Philadelphians was not that He was going to exempt them from future trials, but that He would keep them from harm during those trials. Soldiers in God's Army will participate in spiritual warfare, and even though the battles may be difficult, our General will deliver us. *"My prayer is not that you take them out of the world but that you protect them from the evil one"* (John 17:15, cf. Matt. 6:13).

"that no one can shut" (v. 8). Despite difficult worldly circumstances, believers will emerge victorious by walking through the door that Christ has opened.

There are many places where, seemingly, the Church has little impact. Prevailing society may marginalize or ignore Her message. In American culture, religion tends to be a "private" matter, often with little influence on the general public. One's faith, if expressed at all, is visible for one hour on Sunday mornings. The remaining 167 hours of the week are dominated by the concerns of business and industry or by other cultural phenomena. The "separation of Church and State" does not mean the separation of moral influence from the public square, although it is commonly misunderstood to mean just that.

This was the type of culture faced by the church in Philadelphia. The church was faithful, and worked hard bringing the gospel message to bear on the structures of society around it, but met with very little success. In such situations, there are great temptations to give up, and to look for other venues where an impact can be made. But God's message to the church in Philadelphia and to local churches today that can relate to her struggle is: "continue to persevere." Don't give up. *"Press on toward the goal to win the prize for which God has called* (us) *heavenward in Christ Jesus"* (Phil. 3:14). "It is not the size or strength of a church that determines its ministry, but faith in the call and command of the Lord."[49]

Laodicea ... (3:14-22)

In recent years, the United States government has made extensive use of the armed forces reserve. Thousands of men and women have been ordered to leave civilian jobs, muster with their respective units, and participate in extended overseas deployments. For many, this has come as a great shock. What was once considered as an opportunity to get away from the office one weekend per month and two weeks during the summer (while earning a nice paycheck for their efforts), has now become an obligation to go to war. Not a

---

[49]Wiersbe, 42.

few Reservists are facing a reality they had long denied: that they are men and women who might be called upon to defend their nation. Most have met their responsibilities with honor, but some have acted very surprised when asked to pick up arms, as if they did not realize what the Reserves were all about. Others have tried to renege on their obligations. The church in Laodicea was in denial about its responsibilities to help advance the kingdom of God. Members were called to serve in the Lord's Army, but they were apathetic. The Laodiceans enjoyed picking up their paychecks, but they did not relish the thought of forsaking the comforts of home.

Laodicea was an inland valley city, located at the juncture of two major trade routes. It was the wealthiest of the seven cities of Revelation, well known for a type of sheep that produced soft, glossy black wool; for a prosperous banking industry; and for a famous medical school that was renowned for its medicinal ointments in general, and a very effective eye-salve in particular. The city had a severe water problem, with most of its water supply coming through stone pipes from springs lying six miles to the south.[50]

With the city's water situation in mind, John rebuked the church for being "lukewarm" about the gospel (v. 19; c.f. Prov. 3:11-12; Heb. 12:5-6). Hieropolis, six miles to the north, was famous for her therapeutic hot springs; while Colossae, equally well known for her refreshing springs of cold, pure water, was located ten miles away. By the time these waters had flowed south to Laodicea, however, they had turned lukewarm. When an "unsuspecting visitor" came to the city and drank from the "sickly insipid water seeping over the slimy rock," he or she most certainly would spit it out upon the ground.[51]

Reservists are called upon to support their Active Duty brothers and sisters. A cup of hot coffee or soup can rejuvenate an exhausted, chilled warrior. A cold beverage has the same effect on one who has been fighting in hot, humid conditions. The

---

[50]Mounce, 122-123
[51]Ibid., 125.

Laodiceans, however, offered nothing more to slake the spiritual thirst of the men and women serving on the front lines than the lukewarm water already available in their war battered canteens.

The Laodicean church was also rebuked for trusting in worldly riches. It found great pleasure in the trinkets of the sea beast (n. 18:12-19). Despite vast material wealth, the church was *"wretched, pitiful, poor, blind and naked"* (v. 17). Christ's counsel was to *"buy from me gold refined in the fire ... white clothes to wear ... and salve to put on your eyes"* (v.18). The money you make in the banking business will not purchase your salvation on the Day of Judgment. The soft woolen garments you wear will not cover up your iniquities, and the expensive salves produced in your medical schools will not open the eyes of those who are spiritually blind. You are rich in the things of this world, Christ declared, but poor in the things of God.

The Bible is filled with warnings about placing one's trust in money. The Preacher in the Book of Ecclesiastes says, *"Whoever loves money never has money enough"* (Eccles. 5:10). Jesus said, *"it is easier for a camel to go through the eye of a needle than for a rich man to enter the kingdom of God"* (Matt. 19:24). The Apostle Paul writes:

> *People who want to get rich fall into temptation and a trap and into many foolish and harmful desires that plunge men into ruin and destruction. For the love of money is a root of all kinds of evil. Some people, eager for money, have wandered from the faith and pierced themselves with many griefs* (1 Tim. 6:9-10; cf. James 5:3).

It is not that riches themselves are wrong, but when the pursuit of them becomes a consuming passion, it destroys the soul. Are you rich in the things of this world and poor in the things of God, or are you rich in the things of God and poor in the things of this world? The first choice leads to death, the second to life.

Boot Camp

There are many churches today that conduct their meetings in beautiful gothic structures made of stone. Stained glass windows surround the sanctuary with an array of colors that are breathtaking. The voices of professional singers and musicians echo through the halls of worship on Sunday mornings, and endowments are in place to ensure maintenance for the next millennium. But tragically, there is no passion for the gospel. There is more concern over a soiled carpet or a broken window than there is over the spiritual state of the men and women who worship there. A few coins might be tossed in the direction of the poor, but the focus is totally on the beauty of ecclesiastical properties. Such is the condition of many churches around the world today; such was the state of the church in Laodicea long ago.

Christ called the Laodiceans to repentance, yet His words are laced with compassion. *"Here I am! I stand at the door and knock. If anyone hears my voice and opens the door, I will come in and eat with him, and he with me"* (v. 20). Regardless of how far one might be from the kingdom of God, there is always hope. The Commanding Officer of a company at boot camp often will call the most wayward of recruits into his or her office to offer a last chance at success. Sometimes a direct appeal from the commander is all that a young man or woman will need in order to turn things around and get on the right track. Even though the Laodiceans were far from the kingdom, Christ appealed to the door of their hearts. But for Him to come in and dine, the door must be opened from the inside.

To him who overcomes[52]... (3:21)

Graduation from boot camp is an elaborate affair. Family and friends are invited. Military bands perform the national anthem and other patriotic numbers. Flags are displayed. Dress uniforms are worn. There are parades, the sounding of canon shots, speeches by dignitaries, and awards. Those who graduate are given liberty, and then

---

[52] The Greek word translated as "him who overcomes," is a military term that means "to conquer," or "to come off victorious."

assigned to combat units where they are entrusted with the nation's defense. During times of war, graduation from boot camp is a serious and sobering proposition.

The local church is responsible for recruiting and equipping soldiers for God's Army. In every church there are many who serve as warriors for the Most High, but there will be some who say all of the right words and go through all of the appropriate motions, without having surrendered their hearts to the authority of the Commander of Troops (n. Matt. 7:21-23). Unless these repent and receive the grace of God, they will remain in boot camp forever, and will never join the Lord's Army. In fact, they stand in opposition to the Heavenly Army, and will experience the wrath and judgment revealed in the Book of Revelation.

"Overcomers" are those who believe in the Lord Jesus Christ (n. 1 John 5:5). They have victory over the temptations of the red dragon, the sea beast, and the earth beast. They are graduates from God's boot camp, the true leaders of the local church, and foot soldiers in the Army of God. Overcomers are found in each of the seven churches of Revelation. They are the ones who recognize their own sinfulness and know that Christ died on a cross for them. Out of gratitude for what the great General has done, soldiers in God's Army faithfully live out His commands, and teach them to others. They trust God, even in the most fearful of situations, and will one day be rewarded for their efforts. Graduates from God's boot camp inherit the kingdom of God.

Graduates from the Ephesian boot camp, those who return to their first love, will *"eat from the tree of life"* (2:7). When Adam and Eve rebelled against God, the human race was expelled from the Garden of Eden and prohibited access to this tree (Gen. 3:24). The victory of Jesus Christ, however, destroyed the ancient curse and reopened the Garden for all who believe (22:2).

Graduates in Smyrna, even those put to death for their faith, will *"not be hurt ... by the second death"* (2:11; cf. 20:6). The first death is physical. Adam died, Eve died, and anyone who sins will undergo the same fate (Gen. 2:17; Rom. 5:12). This is a painful reality of the world in which we live. The second death is spiritual, and like physical death, came about as a result of Adam's rebellion. The Book of Revelation uses the imagery of a *"lake of fire"* (20:14; 21:8) to describe spiritual death, but the Scriptures tell us that this horrible reality can be overcome by trusting Jesus Christ. In a conversation with the great Jewish leader Nicodemus, Jesus said, *"I tell you the truth, no one can see the kingdom of God unless he is born again"* (John 3:3). Christ offers spiritual rebirth to those who join His Army. If you are born only once (physically), you will die twice (physically and spiritually), but if you are born twice (spiritually as well as physically) you will only die once (physically). Those who reject the gracious offer of our Heavenly General will taste the second death, an eternity of punishment in the lake of fire.

Graduates in Pergamum, those who do not eat food sacrificed to idols, will be given *"some of the hidden manna"* (2:17). Manna from heaven sustained the people of God for forty years in the wilderness (Exod. 16:4; Ps. 78:24), but Jesus said, *"it is my Father who gives you the true bread from heaven,"* and that, *"I am the bread of life. He who comes to me will never go hungry, and he who believes in me will never be thirsty"* (John 6:32, 35). There will be no more hunger in the kingdom of God.

The graduates in Pergamum will also receive *"a white stone with a new name written on it"* (2:17). Mounce suggests that at the time Revelation was written, white stones were used for many purposes. They served as tokens for admission to banquets. "They were distributed to the poor ... to insure a regular supply of corn, given to the victor at games, and to gladiators who had won the admiration of the public and had been allowed to retire from further combat."[53] Those who serve in the Army of God will be seated at a great banquet table at the end of time (19:9), and will one day retire from the combat of this world (14:13).

To each of the graduates of God's boot camp in Thyatira, to those who do not succumb to the "power" of Jezebel, Christ will grant authority over the nations (n. Matt. 18:18; 19:28; Luke 10:17-20; 22:30; 1 Cor. 6:2) and will *"give ... the morning star"* (2:26-28).

---

[53]Mounce, 99-100.

This latter expression might be a reference to Daniel's prophecy: *"Those who are wise will shine like the brightness of the heavens ... like the stars forever and ever"* (Dan. 12:3), or it may tie in with what Jesus says about Himself, *"I am ... the bright Morning Star"* (22:16). To be sure, blessings come to those who follow Christ. There is the "assurance of the coming dawn, when lamplight will be swallowed up in the light of eternal day."[54]

Graduates in Sardis, those who do not fall asleep on watch, will walk with the Lord, *"dressed in white"* (3:4; cf. 3:18; 4:4; 6:11; 7:13; 19:14). The Psalmist speaks of God clothing *"himself in light as with a garment"* (Ps. 104:2). There is a day coming when God *"will transform our lowly bodies so that they will be like his glorious body"* (Phil. 3:21), and we will appear as Moses and Elijah did on the Mount of Transfiguration (Matt. 17:2-3).

The graduates in Sardis will also have their names written in *"the book of life"* (3:5). Although it is very important to be active in a local church (and that may entail having your name written on a church role), it is far more important to have your name recorded in the book of life. Many of the Biblical authors make mention of this "book" (n. Exod. 32:32; Isa. 4:3; Dan. 12:1; Ps. 69:28; Luke 10:20; Phil. 4:3), and the expression is used on four other occasions in Revelation (13:8, 17:8; 20:12-15; 21:27). Those who place their trust in the Heavenly General will be mustered as "present" on Judgment Day, and will enter the New Jerusalem. On that Day, Jesus will acknowledge those who have served in His Army before His *"Father and his angels"* (3:5). We are not ashamed to testify of our faith in Jesus Christ. As our Lord Himself said,

> *Whoever acknowledges me before men, I will also acknowledge him before my Father in heaven. But whoever disowns me before men, I will disown him before my Father in heaven* (Matt. 10:32-33).

---

[54]Wilcock, 51.

Three promises are extended to the graduates of God's boot camp in Philadelphia (3:12), to those who patiently endure the slings of the enemy: 1) they will become pillars in the temple of God, a very appealing image in this earthquake prone city; 2) the name of God and the name of the city of God will be written upon them. Like the high priests of Old Testament Israel, followers of the Heavenly General will be set apart by the words "*HOLY TO THE LORD*" (Exod. 28:36-38; cf. 7:3; 14:1; 22:4); and 3) they will be given new names. Just as the city itself was given a new name upon rising out of the rubble, believers will be blessed with new names when the kingdom of God comes in its fullness. Many men and women in the Bible experienced a name change upon encountering the Lord of hosts: Abram became Abraham; Jacob became Israel; Simon became Peter, and Saul became Paul.

Graduates from the Laodicean boot camp, those who shook off their apathy and became passionate about their faith, were given the right to sit with Jesus Christ upon His throne. Our General said, "*I tell you the truth, at the renewal of all things, when the Son of Man sits on his glorious throne, you who have followed me will also sit on twelve thrones, judging the twelve tribes of Israel*" (Matt. 19:28; cf. 2 Tim. 2:12).

If you follow Jesus Christ, you are already an overcomer. You are a graduate from God's boot camp, currently engaged in spiritual warfare. All of the rewards, listed above, are yours. You may have received some of them already, but others are yet to be claimed. In human warfare, the results are always uncertain, but those who serve in God's Army are guaranteed victory. The anthem for the great army of nonviolent resisters in the American South of the 1960's was, "We Shall Overcome," but those who serve Christ have overcome already.[55] As we continue our study through the Book of Revelation, we shall see how, in the midst of ferocious battle, God protects His people.

---

[55] Eller, *War and Peace*, 52.

CHAPTER 3

CAPTAIN'S ON THE BRIDGE
(Revelation 4:1-5:14)

A prince should assume personal command and captain his troops himself[56]
  - Machiavelli

After this ... (4:1)
Following graduation from boot camp, the newly initiated warrior will receive additional specialized training, but it will not be long before he reports to his first command. For a brand new sailor, reporting aboard a ship at sea can be a very bewildering experience. Even though he or she went through boot camp, and has some idea of what is to come, the reality of shipboard life hits home. Language learned in the sterile environment of a classroom is spoken fluently on board. A door is a "hatch," a wall is a "bulkhead," and a toilet is a "head." Instead of "rooms," the ship has "compartments," and most have very strange names. The new sailor must be able to locate the Combat Information Center, after-steering, and the boatswain's locker. There are some fascinating individuals with whom our friend must become acquainted: the "SMO" (Senior

---
[56] Niccolo Machiavelli, *The Prince*, trans. George Bull (United States of America: Penguin Books, 1982), 78.

Captain's on the Bridge

Medical Officer), the "CHENG" (Chief Engineer), the "OHO" (Ordnance Handling Officer), and the "SUPPO" (Supply Officer), among others.

All of the power for a warship is consolidated on the bridge. From there, the ship is safely navigated, control is maintained over electronic emissions, and orders are given to launch weapons. A vast array of bells, whistles, lights, and sounds – although confusing to the new sailor – bring order and stability to the entire vessel. Prominently located on either wing of the bridge is the captain's chair, and only the commanding officer is permitted to sit in it.

After John had written down Christ's initial instructions to each of the seven churches, he notices *"a door standing open in heaven."* On behalf of all of God's people, he is about to have glimpse of the throne room of God, a war room as it were. From this command center, all power in heaven and on earth is consolidated, and from here war is waged. The sights and sounds John is about to see are strange and confusing, but through it all he continues writing in order that the people of God throughout the ages might be strengthened and comforted.

"Come up here ..." (4:1)
John is summoned to heaven by a voice that sounds like a trumpet. This is the same voice he heard when Christ first appeared to him on Patmos (1:10). Following chapter three, the word "church" does not appear again until chapter 22. As a result, many Christians are convinced that sometime very soon, the Church will be "raptured" out of this world, leaving only unbelievers and the nation of Israel behind.[57] These will be forced to endure the "Great Tribulation," a series of events described in chapters 4-19 of Revelation.

But there will be no avoiding the draft; Christians are obligated to serve in the Lord's Army. The message of the Apocalypse is not that God will spare us from battle, but that He will protect us in the midst of it. Although many Christians find a great deal of comfort in the idea of a "rapture," our true consolation rests in the fact that Jesus Christ is coming back again to set up a new heaven and a new earth.

As we shall see, even though the word "church" is not used, there are many symbolic references to the people of God throughout chapters 4-19.[58] The verse at which we are looking says that *John*, not the Church, was summoned to heaven. He was allowed to see *"what must take place"* in order to bring encouragement to those who follow Jesus Christ. Nowhere in the Bible can the reader find a passage of Scripture that substantiates the concept of believers being "snatched" out of this world, leaving unbelievers behind for a seven-year period.[59] "Rapture" theology,[60] quite popular in the market place, is not part of God's war plan.

---

[57]C. I. Scofield, *The Oxford NIV Scofield Study Bible*, ed. C.I. Scofield (New York: Oxford University Press, 1984), 1318, declares: 'Beginning with 4:1 the viewpoint of John is from heaven. As the word "church" does not appear again in Revelation until 22:16, the catching up of John from earth to heaven has been taken to be a symbolic representation of the translation of the Church as occurring before the events of the tribulation described in chs. 6-19.'

[58]Note comments on the 144,000 (pp. 101-104), the two witnesses (pp. 117-120), and the woman clothed with the sun (p. 120-121).

[59]In traditional Christian theology, passages such as 1 Th. 4:16-17 have been viewed as different perspectives on the Second Coming of Christ. See footnote 48 and comments on pp. 139-144 for further insight.

[60]Dave MacPherson, *The Incredible Cover-up,* (Plainfield, New Jersey: Logos International, 1975), 7, 11, traces the rise of "rapture" theology to a spiritual movement that broke out in England around 1830, where the utterances of a young woman 'speaking in tongues, announced the "revelation" that the true church would be caught up (raptured) to heaven before the tribulation and before Christ's return to earth.'

there before me was a throne ... (4:2)
Not unlike the captain's chair on the bridge of a ship, the throne in heaven is the focus of attention. It is the seat of power from which all action emanates. The word "throne" occurs thirty-five times in the Book of Revelation. Each time we encounter the word and read of the One seated upon it, we are reminded of the absolute sovereignty of the Almighty. Even though we cannot see Him, He rules over the heavens and the earth.

the one who sat there ... (4:3)
John was given a glimpse of God, our Heavenly King. His vision was similar to that of earlier prophets who recorded what they had seen (n. Isa. 6:1-5; Ezek. 1; Dan. 7:9-10; 1 Kings 22:19; cf. Exod. 33:12-23; 2 Cor. 12:2-4). God's *"appearance of jasper and carnelian"* recalls the beautiful gems that adorned the breastpiece of Old Testament high priests (Exod. 28:17-20), as well as the beauty of the guardian cherub in Ezekiel's prophecy (Ezek. 28:13). Jasper is clear in color, while carnelian (or sardius) is red. *"A rainbow, resembling an emerald, encircled the throne."* When God hung the rainbow in the clouds for Noah it was accompanied by the promise: *"Never again will the waters become a flood to destroy all life"* (Gen. 9:15). Here, the bow is complete, and the promises of life and justice are far greater.

twenty-four elders ... (4:4)
As the commanding officer of a ship is supported in his work by department heads, division officers, and other support staff, several circles of influence surround God's throne in heaven. In its very center are *"four living creatures"* (4:6). Immediately before it are *"the seven spirits of God"* (4:5).[61] Surrounding the throne are *"twenty-four elders"* (4:4), while encircling it are *"many angels, numbering thousands upon thousands, and ten thousand times ten thousand"* (5:11).

---
[61] See comments on p. 36-37.

The twenty-four elders play a prominent role in the Book of Revelation (5:8, 14; 11:16; 19:4). On each occasion, they are seen falling down before the throne and worshiping the King who is seated upon it. Some scholars feel that the twenty-four elders symbolically represent all of God's people, the leaders of the twelve tribes of Old Testament Israel and the twelve Apostles of the New Testament Church (n. 21:12-14). Others believe that the twenty-four elders may be an exalted angelic order, the heavenly reality behind the "twenty-four priestly and the twenty-four Levitical orders" found in the Old Testament (1 Chron. 24:4; 25:9-13; cf. 1 Chron. 23:4; Luke 1:5-9).

lightning, rumblings and peals of thunder ... (4:5)
Our King commands the forces of nature. Mt. Sinai rocked with thunder and lightning when He prepared to speak with Moses (Exod. 19:16). *"Peals of thunder, rumblings, flashes of lightning and an earthquake"* also accompanied the opening of the seventh seal (8:5), the sounding of the seventh trumpet (11:19), and the pouring out of the seventh bowl (16:18).

a sea of glass, clear as crystal ... (4:6)
Heaven is the ultimate reality. The sea of glass was mentioned at creation when God said, *"Let there be an expanse between the waters to separate water from water"* (Gen. 1:6). Ezekiel wrote about it subsequent to his visions of God at the Kebar River (Ezek. 1:22), and Daniel's *"river of fire"* (Dan. 7:10) offers yet another description of the crystalline sea before the throne of our King.

four living creatures ... (4:6-8)
The similarities between the creatures that John is describing, the four-winged cherubim of Ezekiel chapter one, and the six-winged seraphim of Isaiah chapter six are noteworthy. These are, no doubt, the same. The differences in the three accounts may be due to the poverty of human language to offer accurate descriptions of heavenly realities (n. 2 Cor. 12:4). The appearance of these creatures is

enlightening: A lion is king of the beasts, the ox is supreme among domesticated animals, man has dominion over all the earth, while the eagle rules over the birds of the air. These four creatures, at the heart of God's throne, symbolize the pinnacle of His creative power. They spend their time in worship; day and night the creatures cry out:

> Holy, holy, holy
> is the Lord God Almighty,
> who was, and is, and is to come
> (cf. Isa. 6:3)

glory, honor and thanks to him who sits on the throne ... (4:9) One of the commands our King issues to his people is: "*Remember the Sabbath day by keeping it holy*" (Exod. 20:8). We disobey this to our own detriment. We work too hard, and often place our own agenda before God's. Could it be that the efficiency of our work decreases and the number of visits to the psychologist's office increases when we fail to worship? Our souls need rest and refreshment; our spiritual swords need sharpening. When we fail to humble ourselves before the Most High, we often become bitter, angry, or depressed, and lose our effectiveness as spiritual warriors.

In heaven we will be worshiping. The four living creatures are worshiping, the twenty-four elders are worshiping, and myriad angels surrounding the throne join in. Our praises mingle with theirs, and one day we will physically join them. The Book of Revelation is the source of many of our greatest hymns and worship choruses. The words spoken by the four living creatures in verse eight, and by the twenty-four elders in verse eleven, have inspired two very popular worship songs in our churches today.[62]

---

[62]"Holy, Holy, Holy," text: Reginald Heber, music: John B. Dykes, descant: Gary Rhodes; and "Thou Art Worthy," text and music: Pauline M. Mills, *THE HYMNAL for Worship & Celebration*, (Waco, Texas: WORD MUSIC, 1986), #262, #73.

They lay their crowns before the throne ... (4:10)
Military warriors earn beautifully colored ribbons and shiny, ornate medals for service, honor, and courage. Spiritual warriors also earn crowns. Paul speaks of a *"crown that will last forever"* (1 Cor. 9:25) and of a *"crown of righteousness"* (2 Tim. 4:8). Peter writes of a *"crown of glory that will never fade away"* (1 Peter 5:4). James declares that the one who perseveres under trial will receive a *"crown of life"* (James 1:12). These spiritual crowns are rewards for faithful service, and we will be proud of them. But like the twenty-four elders in Command Central, we are willing to lay down before God those things we cherish most in our lives.

a scroll ... sealed with seven seals ... (5:1)
John's vision of heaven continues into the fifth chapter of Revelation, but a dramatic change takes place. The King seated upon the throne now has a scroll in his right hand (we might refer to this as a "War Scroll"), and all of heaven's attention is focused upon it. Ignore the throne. Pay no mind to the emerald rainbow, the glassy sea, the four living creatures, or the twenty-four elders. Rivet your attention to the sealed scroll. Some equate it to that which was revealed long ago to the prophet Daniel. As the future of the world unfolded before his eyes, Daniel was told to *"seal the words of the scroll until the time of the end"* (Dan. 12:4; cf. Dan. 8:26; 12:9). The time has now come to open it! (A military equivalent of what is transpiring in Revelation chapter five might be that of a "Top Secret" document – an Operations Order – containing battle plans formulated long ago, suddenly being delivered to the officer of the deck[63] underway.)

Others suggest that the scroll is some sort of "title deed" to the Earth. Rosenthall points us to the Old Testament practice of "kinsman redeemer." If a property owner came upon hard times, there was a procedure whereby he was able to mortgage his holdings. Generally, the mortgage agreement took the form of a sealed book

---

[63] Officers of the deck are highly trained men and women who are entrusted with the safe operation of the warship when the captain is not on the bridge.

that would be placed into the hands of the creditor. Later, a legal representative of the original property owner could buy back the book and break the seals.[64] The Book of Leviticus offers some insight:

1. The land is not sold permanently (Lev. 25:23).

2. If someone *"becomes poor and sells some of his property, his nearest relative is to come and redeem what his countryman has sold"* (Lev. 25:25).

3. *"if he does not acquire the means to repay him, what he sold will remain in the possession of the buyer until the Year of Jubilee"* (Lev. 25:28).

On a grand scale, we might suggest that the human race was given dominion over the earth (Gen. 1:26; 2:15), but lost it when Adam rebelled against God. Applying the Leviticus principles of redemption to all of humanity, we might suggest: 1) humans have not lost control of the earth permanently; 2) we need a near relative or a kinsman who can come and redeem that which is lost; and 3) there is a heavenly jubilee coming, where all will be returned to us.[65] The scroll held up high by our King, in the presence of myriad heavenly witnesses, begs the question, "who is worthy to open it?" The earth has been plunged into darkness; her rightful owners are no longer in charge. "Is there a near relative who can come and redeem what has been lost?"

"Who is worthy to break the seals and open the scroll?" (5:2-4)
Any officer of the deck (OOD), upon receiving a "flash" message to execute a Top Secret battle plan, would tremble. Despite all of the training he or she has had, an order to send a warship into

---

[64]Marvin Rosenthall, *The Lamb That Will Roar Like a Lion* (Orlando, FL: ZION'S HOPE, Inc.), audio cassette.
[65]An example of how a "kinsman redeemer" works is found in the Book of Jeremiah. The prophet redeemed a field from his uncle for seventeen shekels of silver. The scroll was signed and sealed in the presence of many witnesses and given to the care of Baruch (32:6-16). Only Jeremiah was entitled to retrieve the scroll, open it, and carry out its provisions on behalf of his uncle.

action needs attention from the commanding officer. The wise OOD would immediately issue an urgent summons, over the ship's speaker system, requesting the captain's presence on the bridge.

In this case, it was a mighty angel who issued the summons, *"Who is worthy to break the seals and open the scroll"* (v. 2)? Where is the Captain of our salvation? Is there anyone in heaven or on earth able to lead us in this final battle, the battle for the redemption of the human race? As John pondered the question, the text tells us that he wept. *"No one was found who was worthy to open the scroll or look inside"* (v. 4).

the Lion ... a Lamb ... (5:5-8)

"Captain's on the bridge!" These words ring out from the boatswain mate of the watch the moment that the commander officer enters. There is a great sense of security when the captain is present. He or she may call for general quarters, a command for all personnel to "man" their battle stations. The ship is thus prepared to execute war plans, with the most qualified warrior in charge.

There was a great sense of relief in heaven when *"the Lion of the tribe of Judah"* (v. 5; cf. Gen. 49:9; Heb. 7:14) entered the throne room. But unlike earthly battles, the outcome of this one had already been decided. As prophesied by Daniel, *"one like a son of man ... approached the Ancient of Days and was led into his presence"* (7:13), and as mentioned by the author of the Book of Hebrews, *"he entered heaven itself ...to appear for us in God's presence"* (9:24), we now see Jesus, returning as a conquering warrior. The Son of God, who had been sent to the earth to drive out *"the prince of this world"* (John 12:31), was now returning in triumph. He had won the battle for human souls on the cross at Calvary. He died for our sins, and on the third day rose from the dead. The Kinsman Redeemer, the One able to open the scroll and break its seals, has come. He paid the purchase price and now rightfully claims what is His own. Jesus, our General, is in charge; the "War Scroll" is in His hands. Jubilee has arrived.

In human war, the outcome is often decided long before combat operations cease. The brutal dictator of a regime can be overthrown and locked up in prison, but his henchman will continue to fight, and the battles can wax bloody. The scroll that Jesus takes from the hand of the King tells us that the outcome of God's war has already been decided. Even though demonic legions continue to wreak havoc upon the earth, Satan has been locked away in the Abyss for a thousand years (20:2; see also comments on pp. 113-114 and 144-146). The land has been redeemed, but squatters must be removed. As the seals are broken, final mop up operations begin. Eventually, the Day of the Lord will arrive, and the earth will be purged of evil forever.

One of the twenty-four elders spoke of the triumph of a *Lion*, but when John looked he saw a *Lamb,* and to the Jewish mindset, a lamb suggests sacrifice. Christ's victory over evil came about not through violence, but through sacrifice. He refused to play Satan's game and respond to violence with violence. The war was over because He laid down His life like a lamb. The power of such sacrifice proved to be lion-like. Jesus is *"the Lamb of God, who takes away the sin of the world"* (John 1:29; 1 Peter 1:19). Christians believe that Jesus fulfills Abraham's prophetic words, *"God himself will provide the lamb for the burnt offering"* (Gen. 22:8), and of Isaiah's prophecy, *"he was led like a lamb to the slaughter"* (Isa. 53:7). This Lion/Lamb is now in charge at the command post. The *"seven horns"* symbolize perfect power, omnipotence. His *"seven eyes"* suggest omniscience, while *"the seven spirits of God sent out into all the earth"* point to omnipresence. No power in heaven or on earth can possibly succeed in squaring off against a Warrior with such formidable attributes.

And they sang a new song ... (5:9-14)
Music is used to encourage the troops. This is why all branches of the armed services have bands affiliated with them. Spiritual warriors also employ music. This is why we sing. When the host of heaven witnessed the entrance of the Lamb into the throne room, they burst out in song:

> *You are worthy to take the scroll and to open its seals,*
> *Because you were slain, and with your blood*
> *you purchased men for God*
> *From every tribe and language and people and nation.*
> *You have made them to be a kingdom*
> *and priests to serve our God,*
> *and they will reign on the earth.*

As Jesus takes the scroll from Him who sits on the throne, all creation rejoices. The four living creatures and the twenty-four elders lead this worship service, prostrating themselves before the Lord of all heaven and earth (5:8). They give glory to God for the redemption He has secured. Millions of angels sing praises to the Lord (v. 11; cf. Dan. 7:10), and then *"every creature in heaven and on earth and under the earth and on the sea"* (v. 13) joins in. As ever-expanding concentric circles on the top of a pond will eventually cover the entire surface, so all of creation resonates with the praises of God as the Lamb takes hold of the scroll. The thundering voices of the four living creatures close this passage of Scripture with a loud *"Amen."* Verily, truly, this is how it is supposed to be. We have languished long enough under the reign of darkness. The rightful King is now in charge, and all of creation is glad.

The Scriptures encourage us to sing (Eph. 5:19-20), and God is pleased, even if we fail to carry a tune. In fact, the expression "make a joyful *noise*" occurs more frequently in the Bible than does the idea of singing melodiously (e.g. Pss. 95:1; 98:4; 100:1). Even though most of us should keep our day jobs, when we sing corporately, as an act of worship, our lives improve and our faces shine. Even voices that are loud and off-key sound vibrant and beautiful when carried along by more gifted voices in the congregation. But the most uplifting of worship services on earth are mere foretastes of what will one day transpire.

The Scriptures also encourage us to be creative and sing new songs. Pity the church so trapped in tradition that it does not allow for a "new song," or for new ways of expressing an old one. When

God works in somebody's life or in the lives of an entire community, a new song is always appropriate. When God delivered Moses and the Israelites, the freed people sang a new song (Exod. 15:1-21). When King David captured the ark of God from the Philistines and returned it to Jerusalem, the whole house of Israel celebrated *"with all their might before the LORD, with songs and harps, lyres, tambourines, sistrums and cymbals"* (2 Sam. 6:5). Songs fill the Bible, telling of the glory and majesty of Almighty God. The entire book of Psalms was a songbook for the nation of Israel (n. Pss. 33:1-3; 40:3; 96; 98; 144:9 and 149:1).

The history of the Church is replete with beautiful hymns and anthems, written by people whose lives were changed by the power of the Holy Spirit. At one time, these songs were new. Many endured the test of time, because the power of their words and melodies were renewed in the lives of generations of subsequent believers. Other "new" songs faded from use, because they no longer resonated with the people of God. But the Most High continues to bring personal victory to individual lives, putting new songs on the lips of changed people. Our churches should be flexible enough to embrace the words and music of those whose lives were changed long ago, as well as the new songs that arise as a result of lives being changed today.

The heavenly choir sings praises to the Lamb because of His glorious victory over the enemy. The words to the song tell of the sacrifice our General has made (again the image of throwing Himself on a grenade comes to mind) in order to bring life to all races and cultures of people. His victory at the cross begins to restore the glory lost in the Garden of Eden. Evil is to be vanquished forever, and even though we presently sing *"the songs of the LORD while in a foreign land"* (Ps. 137:4), there is a day coming when we will sing in the presence of the Lamb Himself.

Chapter 4

JUST CAUSE

(Revelation 6:1-11)

Morally, a failure to respond to massive human catastrophes like that in Somalia would scar the soul of our nation ... But we should consider using military force only in those situations where the stakes warrant, where it can be effective and its application limited in scope and time. As we seek to save lives, we must always be mindful of the lives that we may have to put at risk.[66]
  - President George H. W. Bush

the Lamb opened the first of the seven seals ... (v. 1)
The decision to send a nation to war should be the most agonizing one that political leaders ever make. "War is the hardest place,"[67] a terrible condition that should not be entered into casually. Over the centuries, Church scholars have developed a theology of just war (*jus ad bellum*) that warrants the prayerful consideration any government official tasked with making such an ominous decision. Allen offers a concise summary: 1) just cause, 2) legitimate author-

---

[66]Department of State, "America Must Remain Engaged," 21 December 1992, *Dispatch*, vol. 3, no. 51.
[67]Michael Walzer, *Just and Unjust Wars: A Moral Argument with Historical Illustration* (New York: Basic Books, Inc., 1977), xvii.

ity, 3) last resort, 4) declaration of war aims, 5) proportionality, 6) reasonable chance of success, and 7) right intent.[68] St. Augustine (354-430), Thomas Aquinas (1225-74), and Francisco de Vitoria (c. 1492-1546) are among the most notable contributors to the development of this ethic.[69] What we are looking at in this chapter is the criterion of "just cause." Theologian James Turner Johnson suggests three benchmarks: 1) the recovery of that which has been wrongly taken, 2) the punishment of evil, and 3) the overall defense of the common good.[70] As the Lamb opens the first five seals, God's reasons for war are abundantly clear.

The contents of the seven seals (the first five of which we are addressing in this chapter) are strikingly similar to Jesus' comments in the 24th chapter of Matthew's Gospel (commonly referred to as the "Olivet Discourse") when the disciples asked: *"what will be the sign of your coming and of the end of the age?"* (Matt. 24:3). There is also a very noticeable pattern in the opening of the first four seals. In each case, one of the living creatures that surrounds the throne of God cries out, *"Come"* (6:1, 3, 5, 7).

a white horse ... (vv. 1-2)
The first horseman is mounted on a white steed. He holds a bow, wears a crown, and is *"bent on conquest."* The color white is a symbol of righteousness (n. Matt. 17:2; 28:3; John 20:12; Rev. 3:4). The bow represents military power (n. Jer. 51:56; Hos. 1:5). A crown is a sign of authority.

---

[68]Joseph L. Allen, *War: A Primer for Christians* (Nashville, TN: Abingdon Press, 1991), 36-43. Ethicists have also defined a code for soldiers who are in the midst of war. Walzer describes this as "Justice in war" (*jus in bello*). *Jus in bello* involves discriminating between combatants and noncombatants, while proportionality calibrates violence "to its need for attaining war's end." Gary Wills, review of *Arguing About War*, by Michael Walzer, *The New York Review of Books* 51, No. 18 (November 18, 2004); available from http://www.nybooks.com/articles/17560; Internet.
[69]Lisa Sowle Cahill, *Love Your Enemies: Discipleship, Pacifism, and Just War Theory* (Minneapolis: Fortress Press, 1994), 93.
[70]James Turner Johnson, "Just War, As It Was and Is," *First Things* no. 149 (January 2005): 23.

Some interpretations suggest that this horseman and the one found in Revelation chapter nineteen (v. 16) are the same, none other than "*KING OF KINGS AND LORD OF LORDS.*" Difficulties with this view include: 1) it is Jesus who opens the seal; the rider who springs forth is under His authority, and most importantly, 2) the rider on the white horse in chapter nineteen is destroying evil, whereas the rider in this chapter is lumped in with others who seem bent on perpetrating it.

Others believe this horseman to be the Antichrist. Although there is nothing in the text of Revelation (or anywhere else in the Bible) to suggest it, many Christians believe that the Antichrist will come initially as a man of peace who will later show his true colors and try to conquer everything in sight. But the word "antichrist" does not even appear in the Book of Revelation. In fact, it surfaces only four times in the entire Bible (1 John. 2:18, 22; 4:3; 2 John 1:7), and never in connection with the word "peace."[71]

In keeping with our principles of interpretation, perhaps the rider on the white horse is a symbol of imperialism. Acts of international aggression are often couched in pious sounding platitudes (white, you recall, is the color of "righteousness"), hiding more sinister motives for breaching the territorial integrity of other nations, such as the lust for gold, slaves, or other economic reasons. The far-flung conquests of Rome were designed to spread "*Pax Romana.*" The Crusades were launched with the idea of recapturing the Holy Land from the "infidel." Land was forcibly taken from Native Americans, under the euphemism of "Manifest Destiny." Adolf Hitler needed "*lebensraum*" for his Thousand Year Reich. Imperialism has been around since the fall of Adam and Eve, it manifests itself in the modern era, and it breaks the heart of God. The blatant nature of this sin is just cause for waging war against the powers that trigger it. In Matthew 24, Christ indicated that one of the signs of His coming would be that of nation rising up "*against nation, and kingdom against kingdom*" (Matt. 24:7). This sounds quite similar to the imagery of the white horseman of the

---

[71] For more insight into the "Antichrist," see comments regarding the sea beast, pp. 124-128.

first seal. The living creature who cries out, "*Come*," is appealing to the great Rider of Revelation chapter nineteen to bring an end to the savage ways in which the "*inhabitants of the earth*" (6:10) treat each other.

another horse ... a fiery red one ... (vv. 3-4)
Imperialism leads to war. "*When the Lamb opened the second seal,*" a fiery red horse sprang out whose rider "*was given power to take peace from the earth.*" The large sword in the hand of this horseman leaves little doubt as to the symbolic meaning. Ever since Cain killed Abel, there have been wars on the face of the earth. The philosopher Plato once declared that only the dead have seen an end to it.[72] Christians are not exempt from this horrible scourge, and often find themselves in its midst.

In our broken world, military forces do and must exist, and there are times when war may be the lesser of two evils. The One who is worthy to open the great scroll, however, reminds us that there is a day coming when war will cease. In the Olivet discourse, Jesus declared that there would be "*wars and rumors of wars*" (Matt. 24:6) until the time of His coming, but along with the living creature whose voice accompanied the opening of this seal, the people of God also cry out, "Come!" (cf. Rom. 8:22-23; 2 Cor. 5:2). May there be an end to this scourge. May there be a day when all people can "*beat their swords into plowshares and their spears into pruning hooks*" and no longer train for war (Isa. 2:4).

a black horse ... (vv. 5-6)
Wars lead to famine. The rider who springs forth from the third seal holds "*a pair of scales in his hand.*" As the seal is broken, a voice cried out, "*A quart of wheat for a day's wages, and three quarts of barley for a day's wages, and do not damage the oil and the wine!*" The scales may indicate that food is so scarce everything must be weighed before it is distributed (n. Ezek. 4:16). A quart of wheat is sufficient for the daily needs of any one individual, but the price is

---
[72]*Parade, The Sunday Newspaper Magazine* (May 7, 2000): 7.

exorbitant.[73] Could you imagine spending an entire day's wage to purchase a loaf of bread? Barley, a less-nutritious grain, is cheaper to purchase than wheat, but the price is still astronomical. Many suggest that the reference to oil and wine points to the inequalities that exist between the rich and the poor, and that during times of famine the rich get richer and the poor get poorer. Oil and wine, however, "were not luxuries, but part of the basic commodities of life."[74]

Hunger is an ever-present reality. Following World War I, famines in Germany and Russia, and an accompanying influenza pandemic, killed more people than the war. More recent episodes of starvation in sub-Saharan Africa, much of it brought about by war, have been particularly sad. Christians and non-believers have suffered alongside of each other, and although we should struggle valiantly to ensure that all have enough to eat, the tragic fact is that there will be hunger in our world until the return of Jesus Christ (n. Matt. 26:11). Famine, when caused by human action, is a gross violation of human rights. Warlords, and others who would cause people to suffer in this manner, are driven by demonic, unseen powers. As such, it is just cause for Divine wrath. Jesus' words in the Olivet Discourse, *"there will be famines and earthquakes in various places,"* (Matt. 24:7) parallel what the black horseman symbolizes. As with the opening of the first two seals, this one is also accompanied by the voice of a living creature who cries out, *"Come."* Come, Lord Jesus. Bring on the Day of your wrath, a day when the evils of famine will be gone forever.

a pale horse ... (vv. 7-8)
War and famine are two of many paths that lead us to the pale horse. Its color is that of a lifeless corpse, and none escapes the ominous sound of its hoof beats. "All our life is but a going out to

---

[73]Mounce, 155, tells us that the Roman historian, Cicero, indicates that this price is probably ten to twelve times more expensive than it should have been.
[74] Ibid., 155-156.

the place of execution, to death" (John Donne).[75] "One out of one dies" (George Bernard Shaw).[76] "In this world nothing is certain but death and taxes" (Benjamin Franklin).[77] The rider of this horse is our ultimate enemy; his name is *"Death,"* and his partner *"Hades"* follows closely behind. Both of them await us. Even though the text says *"they were given power over a fourth of the earth,"* the reign of these villains is universal. (It may be that only 25% of humanity will die tragic, violent deaths, but a full 100% will be trampled underfoot.)

During our brief stay upon the earth, we suffer all sorts of little deaths. We lose many things – friends, family members, and material possessions – and when the rider finally comes for us, he takes everything that remains. *"The wages of sin is death"* (Rom. 6:23), and since all of us sin (Rom. 3:23), there is no escaping this hideous horseman and his message of doom.

"Hades" is an unknown character; he is mysterious, and until the time of Christ, no one knew what happened after Death had done his devastating work. But this horseman, like the first three, is now under the authority of our General. It is Jesus who holds *"the keys to death and Hades"* (1:18), and there is a day coming when both will be cast into hell (20:14). *"Listen, I tell you a mystery,"* declares the Apostle Paul (and he is about to resolve some of the mystery concerning this matter of *"hades"*):

> *We will not all sleep, but we will all be changed – in a flash, in the twinkling of an eye, at the last trumpet. For the trumpet will sound, the dead will be raised imperishable, and we will be changed ... "Death has been swallowed up in victory." "Where O death, is your victory? Where, O death, is your sting?" ... thanks be to God! He gives us the victory through our Lord Jesus Christ.* (1 Cor. 15:51-57).

---

[75] Available from http://www.giga-usa.com/quotes/authors/john donne a001.htm; Internet

[76] Available from http://www.christianity.co.nz/life death2.htm; Internet.

[77] Available from http://www.brainyquote.com/quotes/quotes/b/benjaminfr129817.html; Internet.

Jesus disarmed this horseman when He rose from the dead on Easter Sunday. Our General is the first to experience victory over the tyranny of its rider (n. 1 Cor. 15:20; cf. Isa. 25:7-8). Even though we no longer need to tremble at the ominous sound of the pale horseman, Death still causes fear and wreaks havoc in the human community. Holy war is justified in order to exterminate him forever. During the Olivet Discourse, Jesus indicated that even up until the end of time, His disciples would be *"put to death, and ... hated by all nations"* (Matt. 24:9). Like the other three horsemen, our pale nemesis still rides, but his time upon the earth is short. The final living creature cries out, *"Come."* Come, Lord Jesus, you who rose from the dead. Come, and forever rid our world from the curse of this horseman.

the fifth seal ... under the altar ... (vv. 9-10)
As the fifth seal is opened, the action shifts to heaven. (The activity of the four horsemen plays out upon the earth.) We see an altar (cf. Exod. 29:38-41; Lev. 4:7, 18, 25, 30; Phil. 2:17; 2 Tim. 4:6), and underneath it are slain martyrs who cry out, *"How long until you ... avenge our blood?"*

Are these Christians? What is going on? Jesus taught us to forgive, to love, and to pray for those who persecute us (Matt. 5:44), modeling it personally as He hung on the cross (Luke 23:34; cf. Acts 7:60). The Apostle Paul told us not to seek vengeance when wronged (Rom. 12:19). These teachings, and many in a similar vein, are to shape the lives of Christian soldiers as we wage war against *"spiritual forces of evil"* (Eph. 6:12). Yet the martyred souls under the altar seem to be questioning the orders of our Commander. They are crying out for judgment against the *"inhabitants of the earth."* Even though every reference to these "earth people"[78] is in connection with Divine wrath (3:10; 8:13; 12:12; 14:6; 17:2), even though they reject the gospel of Jesus Christ (17:8), gloat over

---

[78] I will often refer to the "inhabitants of the earth" as "earth people," because they place all of their hope in earthly things.

the two witnesses who lie dead in the street (11:10), and worship the beast who rises out of the sea (13:8, 12, 14), the martyrs' attitude seems inappropriate. An explanation is needed.

Later in the Book Revelation we read, *"Blessed are the dead who die in the LORD ... they will rest from their labor"* (14:13). The martyrs under the altar are resting. Their days of soldiering are over, and they are no longer tempted with thoughts of personal vengeance against the earth people. During their time of service, the altar people were faithful in battle. They maintained a testimony,[79] and served honorably. But now they are able to see things from a different perspective. Their voices cry out for justice: "Enough already! When, O God, are you going to bring an end to the evils that ravage the earth – the imperialism, the wars, the famines, the death, and the persecution of your people? How long will this go on?" Their questions are similar to those of the Psalmist who writes, *"How long will the enemy mock you, O God? Will the foe revile your name forever?"* (Ps. 74:10; cf. Ps 79:10; 94:3).

wait a little longer ... (v. 11)
God's answer to the martyrs' question is somewhat puzzling. They were told to *"wait a little longer, until the number of their fellow servants and brothers who were to be killed ... was completed."* In human warfare, lives are lost. If the war is just, it would be foolish to pull out before victory is achieved. Those who died would have given their lives in vain. There could be some sort of parallel in Divine warfare. We serve at God's pleasure. Things are to be done His way, according to His timetable. In addition to the battle that

---

[79] The word "testimony" comes from the Greek word "marturion." Our English word "martyr" is a derivative. In Greek, marturion is one who "bears witness" or "testifies." Used in a court of law, a "martyr" was someone who testified to a truth. So many early Christians were put to death because of their testimony about Jesus that the word "martyr" eventually changed meaning. A martyr is now someone who dies for a passionately held cause. The images of John exiled on the island of Patmos because of the *"testimony of Jesus"* (1:9), of those under the altar *"slain because of the word of God and the testimony they had maintained"* (6:9), and of souls *"who had been beheaded because of their testimony for Jesus"* (20:4) show why the word took on the meaning it did.

rages within us, our war also involves sharing the gospel with the earth people. In doing this, we may encounter world and life views different from our own; there may be casualties as we share our faith, but we persevere in our assignment, knowing that God's word will not return empty (Isa. 55:11).

God is very patient. He wants as many earth people as possible to enter His kingdom. Sometimes He uses tragedy, even martyrdom, to drive home the message of eternal life. The cry of the martyrs under the altar is not unlike the cries of the four living creatures. All are longing for the Day of the Lord. The martyrs are asking, "How long will you allow this persecution of your people to continue?" Each of the living creatures posed the same question when he cried out, "Come." "Come, Lord Jesus, bring an end to the imperialism, to war, famine, and death." But God says to the martyrs, and to each of the living creatures, "Not yet. I want to bring more of the earth people into my kingdom. There is just cause for my wrath, and justice will come. My kingdom will rule over the kingdoms of this world, but have patience; wait just a bit longer." Peter's words are not unlike these thoughts when he wrote:

> *The Lord is not slow in keeping his promise, as some understand slowness. He is patient with you, not wanting anyone to perish, but everyone to come to repentance. But the day of the Lord will come like a thief. The heavens will disappear with a roar; the elements will be destroyed by fire, and the earth and everything in it will be laid bare* (2 Pet. 3:9-10).

As the ravages of the four horsemen continue until the Day of the Lord, so also the persecution of His people. In the Olivet discourse, our General stated, "*you will be handed over to be persecuted ... you will be hated by all nations because of me ... and then the end will come*" (Matt. 24:9, 14).

Often the men and women who serve in earthly armies do not know all of the reasons why they are being sent into harm's way. Within certain limits, part of being a soldier involves trusting in the wisdom of those who have the power to declare war. Only after combat operations begin (or after the war ends) do the reasons become evident. As John looked in at Command Central in Revelation chapter four, he knew that a war was in progress. When Christ emerged upon the scene in chapter five, John and the rest of the Heavenly Army knew that a mortal wound had been inflicted on the enemy (n. Col. 2:15). As the great General of the Armies took the scroll and began opening the seals, the reasons for this war were abundantly clear.

Imperialism, war, famine, death, and persecution of the righteous are results of the enemy's pernicious influence. All of these things are evil; each has wrongly taken from the human community, has harmed the common good, and serves as just cause for divine warfare. A loving God who is holy and just will not allow this to continue. Our General has already begun the final war that will destroy these evils, restore the land to its rightful owners, and reestablish the common good. The victory that took place at the cross crushed the serpent's head, and even though the people of God still suffer (a rattlesnake, though mortally wounded, can still destroy), there is great hope. D-Day has already happened. The War Scroll is in the Lord's hand, but there are many more battles yet to transpire before the final peace is ushered in. The cry of the living creatures and the appeal of the martyrs under the altar are voices calling out for the "not yet" part of the kingdom. When the sixth seal is opened, however, the great Day of the Lord will begin. The kingdom that is "not yet" will arrive, and the world as we know it now will be changed forever.

Situational update
Thus far in our study, we have looked at the "already" part of the battle in which the Lord Jesus Christ (our General) and His servants (Christian soldiers) have been involved. We spoke of the enemy's resounding defeat at the cross, but also of battles that still

rage. If you are a follower of Jesus Christ, you were, at one point, recruited into the Army of the Most High. As a graduate from boot camp, you were commissioned to recruit others into this Army and mold them into honorable soldiers. Our friend John has taken us into Command Central where we were able to witness the unfolding war, and the sacrifices that were made by those who went before us. In the next few chapters, we begin to focus on the "Day of the Lord," that final battle which will end our warfare forever, and result in a lasting peace.

Up until this point, we have looked at the Book of Revelation in a somewhat linear fashion, but now we begin to jump around. In chapter five, the Commanding General speaks to His troops. In chapter six we look closely at the major combatants. In chapter seven the final battle unfolds, while in chapter eight the last judgment and a lasting peace are ushered in.

Chapter 5

SCHOOL CIRCLE

(Revelation 7, 10, 13:9-10; 14:12-13; 15; 16:15; 20:1-6)

Then Jesus came to them and said, "...And surely I am with you always, to the very end of the age."
   - Matthew 28:18, 20

144,000 from all the tribes of Israel ... (7:1-17)
There are many Christians who believe that sometime in the near future, 144,000 Jews – 12,000 from each of the tribes of Israel – will be converted to Christ during a terrible period in human history known as the Great Tribulation.[80] These will receive a protective seal upon their foreheads, and will be spared the outpouring of wrath that will take place at that time. Unfortunately, there are several problems with this "literal" method of interpretation.

First of all, there are no Jews alive today who can trace their lineage to any of the twelve tribes. When the Assyrians and the Babylonians overran the Northern and Southern kingdoms of ancient Israel and Judah, genealogical connections were broken. Secondly, the listing of the twelve tribes in Revelation chapter seven does not match anything found in the Old Testament. The tribe of Dan is noticeably missing while the "tribes" Levi and Joseph are additions (cf. Num. 1). Third, the very precise number of "12,000," for each of the tribes raises a red flag. Wilcock suggests it is a

---
[80]See footnote 48.

"suspiciously tidy sort of number ... more likely to be a symbol than a statistic."[81] Finally, the word "Israel," as used in many places in the New Testament (and probably in this passage), refers to men and women who believe in Jesus Christ, both Jew and Gentile.[82]

A commonly held point of view is that there are two groups of individuals mentioned in this passage: 1) 144,000 from the twelve tribes of Israel (vv. 1-8), and 2) a large multitude that came out of great tribulation (vv. 9-17). A more probable scenario, however, is that these verses offer two perspectives on the same group. In verse four, John *heard* the number of those who were sealed, while in verse nine, he *sees* a "*great multitude that no one could count, from every nation, tribe, people and language.*" Smith suggests that the "144,000 are the whole community of the faithful in their earthly pilgrimage, sealed by God and protected, as they prepare to do battle against all anti-God powers. The vast innumerable throng in the second half of the chapter (7:9-17) are the same faithful people portrayed at the beginning of the chapter. However, we now view them as standing before God at the end and goal of all their hard journeying. Their warfare is now ended."[83]

The "*great multitude ... standing before the throne and in front of the Lamb*" (v. 9) suggests a "school circle." In human warfare, the commanding officer of a unit may call for a school circle when he or she wishes to speak directly to the troops. The formality, so

---

[81] Wilcock, 80.
[82] The word "Israel" is a Hebrew word that means, "he struggles with God." Throughout Scripture it is used in many different ways. "Israel" was the name that God gave to the Patriarch Jacob (Gen. 32:28); it was the name given to the race of people who descended from him (Exod. 6:7), and it was also the name of the Northern Kingdom (2 Chron. 10:19). In the New Testament, "Israel" often refers to all who believe in Jesus Christ, both Jew and Gentile (Rom. 11:11-27; Gal. 6:16; Eph. 2:11-14; cf. Isa. 66:18-21; Rom. 2:29; Phil. 3:3; James. 1:1; 1 Pet. 2:9; Rev. 2:9; 3:9). The Church Fathers understood "Israel" in this sense. Justin Martyr, for example, who lived from AD 100-165, in *Dialogue with Trypho*, wrote: "we who obey the precepts of Christ ...in reality are, Jacob and Israel and Juda and Joseph and David and true children of God" (Thomas B. Falls, *The Writings of Saint Justin Martyr*, New York: Christian Heritage, Inc., 1948, 339-340).
[83] Robert Smith, *Apocalypse: A Commentary on Revelation in Words and Images* (Collegeville, Minnesota: The Liturgical Press, 2000), 42.

evident in most aspects of military life, is relaxed, and the soldiers gather around their leader. The circle often takes place before or after hard training or during periods of "down time" in combat. It is used to keep warriors informed and to encourage them. A muster would not be taken at such a time.

The large number of spiritual warriors that John saw gathered around our General was impossible to count. A voice told him the number was 144,000. The troops, in this case, are *"the servants of our God"* (v. 3), identified by a seal on their foreheads.[84] The New Testament informs us that Christians are *"marked ... with a seal"* (Eph. 1:13), while a very interesting Old Testament passage refers to an angelic being who marked the foreheads of faithful Jews (Eze. 9:4-6). Some of the "sealed" troops of Revelation 7, Old Testament Jews and the souls of those under the altar in chapter six, have

---

[84]The seal mentioned in Revelation chapter seven should not be confused with the mark of the beast (n. Rev. 13:16-17; 14:11; 16:2; 19:20). This one is of Divine origin, protecting those who are sealed from spiritual demise, and from the Day of God's wrath.

already completed their earthly deployments. Others, like us, are still in combat, struggling to *"take captive every thought to make it obedient to Christ"* (2 Cor. 10:5).

Since the descendants of Abraham are to be as numerous as the stars of heaven (Gen. 15:5) or as the grains of sand along the seashore (Gen. 32:12), and since both Jews and Christians are descendants of Abraham (n. Gal. 3:29); the number "144,000" is most likely a symbol used to describe such a vast multitude. 144,000 is the "number" for all of the servants of God, in both Old and New Testaments, past, present, and future. Twelve is the number of tribes in the Old Testament, and the number of Apostles in the New (n. 21:12-14). Like the number "seven," "one thousand" also appears to be a symbol of perfection or completion.[85] In multiplying these numbers, 12 x 12 x 1000, one arrives at the fascinating figure of 144,000.

The school circle conducted in Revelation chapter seven occurs during a pause in the action between the sixth and the seventh seals. When the sixth seal is opened (we will look at this on page 146), one could say, "All hell breaks loose." Kings and princes, the rich and the poor, slaves and free will cry out: *"the great day of ... wrath has come ... who can stand?"* (6:17). Our General, in the midst of horrible warfare, reminds His people that they will indeed stand. He is leading us to a land where there will be no more hunger or thirst (v. 16), to a place where we will drink from *"springs of living water,"* and where every tear will be wiped from our eyes (v. 17). In the midst of horrible combat, God uses the school circle to comfort us, and to remind us to remain faithful.

A Mighty Angel (10:1-11)[86]
In the battle for human souls, we are assisted by angelic beings, *"ministering spirits sent to serve those who will inherit salvation"* (Heb. 1:14). (One might say that these angels constitute a shadow army

---

[85] God, for example, owns *"the cattle on a thousand hills"* (Ps. 50:10), and shows love *"to a thousand generations"* (Exod. 20:6; Deut. 5:10; 7:9; cf. Ps. 90:4; 2 Pet. 3:8).

[86] The reader should be reminded of the principle of "flashback." We will return to the events of Revelation 8-9 in chapter seven, "The Day of the Lord," after tracing the "school circle" theme.

– Special Ops – unseen by human flesh, yet very much involved in combat operations.) The Book of Revelation is filled with their descriptions. Most serve in the Army of the Most High, but some have rebelled against Him and are headed for certain destruction.

There are seven types of angels in the Apocalypse: *Messenger angels*, such as the one speaking to John (1:1; 22:8), bring God's Word to the human community; *Guardian angels*, like those who hold back four winds of judgment (7:1-3), protect the people of God; *Worship angels* (5:11) surround the throne of God, and assist us in our feeble efforts at praise; the voices of *Divine heralds* resound throughout the heavens, announcing the glorious triumphs of the great Heavenly Warrior (5:2; 14: 6-9; 19:17); *Fallen angels* wage war against our General and against those who would keep His commandments (12:17); *Warrior angels* are at the "tip of the spear," engaging and defeating the Devil and his minions (12:7); while *Angels of judgment* serve to punish those who are the objects of God's wrath (14:17-19). See Appendix A for further insight into the angels of the Apocalypse.

The "*mighty angel coming down from heaven*" (v. 1) is a Divine herald. He has a scroll in his hand,[87] and stands with one foot on the sea and the other on land (cf. Ezek.1: 26-3:15). The angel 'swore by him who lives for ever and ever (n. Dan. 12:7) ... and said, "There will be no more delay!"' (v. 6). Up until this point, John has been a passive observer of the unfolding drama of the Apocalypse, but now he is called to participate in the action. He is told to eat the scroll, which tastes sweet, but in his stomach turns sour. He is then commanded to "*prophesy again about many peoples, nations, languages and kings*" (v. 11).

---

[87]Some scholars believe that this little scroll is the same one described in Revelation 5. Smith, 57, suggests that its contents are revealed in 11:1-19, and understands the entire interlude (10:1-11:19) as a "a kind of Book of Revelation in miniature."

In Revelation chapter seven, between the opening of the sixth and seventh *seals*, during a "down time" in the midst of heavy combat operations, God conducts a school circle with 144,000 warriors from the tribes of Israel. These are reminded that, "*Salvation* (victory) *belongs to our God*" (7:10), and that a day is coming when warfare will cease. The action in this chapter takes place between the sounding of the sixth and seventh *trumpets*. It also occurs during a "down time." It may be that John is describing the very same school circle mentioned in chapter seven. In this case, however, through the mediations of a mighty angel, our General is exhorting the troops to persevere in battle.

The scroll tasted sweet in John's mouth because he was allowed to see a vision of the future, where the cries of those under the altar would be answered, and where justice would prevail upon the earth. But his stomach turned sour when he realized that combat operations were not yet over. Even though the angel cried out, "*there will be no more delay*" (v. 6), it seems (from our perspective, anyway) that there is.[88] John is to return to the place from which he came, and like Ezekiel before him, must continue to bring the message of the kingdom of God to a world that is rebellious, obstinate, and stubborn (Ezek. 2:4). The Church is tasked with the same responsibility. As individual believers, we experience great joy in devouring the contents of the little scroll, but we are saddened as we reflect upon the state of our world and upon the hardness of the human heart. A great chasm exists between sinful humanity and a holy God, and the mission that has been entrusted to us is sobering.

We, as members of the Church, are responsible for carrying out the Great Commission, that of making "*disciples of all nations*" (Matt. 28:19). Doing this is both a great privilege and a difficult task. There are moments we greatly savor as we see men, women, and

---

[88] Vernard Eller, *The Most Revealing Book*, 113, suggests that 'the holding off of the eschaton is a mark of God's grace, his granting men time for repentance. Nevertheless ... the time *will* come – will *have* to come – when the whistle blows, "Sorry, time has run out; the ball game is over!" John ... is not one of these moderns who believe that human history never will involve an accounting but will simply run on forever.'

children come to the saving knowledge of Jesus Christ, bringing their considerable influence to bear upon the institutions of our world. But the little scroll can sour in our bellies as we see the daunting task that remains before us. It is often difficult to be loyal to our commission. Even within the institutional church, there are times when "*men will not put up with sound doctrine…(when) They will turn their ears away from the truth and turn aside to myths*" (2 Tim. 4:2-4). The mighty angel reminds the people of God to continue fighting the good fight; there is a day coming when warfare will cease, and the "*mystery of God will be accomplished*" (v. 7).[89]

Blessed is he who stays awake (16:15)
Perhaps the reader has noticed a pattern. (If not, the chart on the following page should be of assistance.) In between the sixth (6:12-17) and seventh seals (8:1-5), our Commander speaks words of comfort to the troops (7:1-17). In between the sixth (9:13-21) and seventh trumpets (11:15), He urges perseverance (10:1-11). Now, between the sixth (16:12-14) and seventh bowls (16:17-21), we hear the words of exhortation: "*Behold, I come like a thief! Blessed is he who stays awake.*" This is a call to vigilance.

---

[89]There are a lot of "mysteries" that will be understood fully when the end shall come: 1) Rom. 11:25 – "*I do not want you to be ignorant of this mystery … Israel has experienced a hardening in part until the full number of Gentiles has come in,*" 2) 1 Cor. 15:51-52 – "*Listen, I tell you a mystery: We will not all sleep, but we will all be changed – in a flash in the twinkling of an eye,*" 3) Eph. 3:6 – "*This mystery is that through the gospel the Gentiles are heirs together with Israel,*" 4) Eph 5:32 – "*This is a profound mystery – but I am talking about Christ and the church,*" and 5) 2 Thess. 2:7, NKJV – "*For the mystery of lawlessness is already at work; only He who now restrains will do so until He is taken out of the way.*" We have considerable insight into these mysteries already, but when the seventh trumpet sounds and Christ returns, even those things we do not understand will become clear in our minds.

Seal #	Trumpet #	Bowl #
1—the white horse (6:1-2)	1 – hail/blood/fire upon the earth (8:7)	1 – poured out on the land (16:2)
2—the red horse (6:3-4)	2 – fiery mountain cast into the sea (8:8-9)	2 – poured out on the sea (16:3)
3—the black horse (6:5-6)	3 – "Wormwood" star falls from the sky (8:10-11)	3 – poured out on the rivers (16:4-7)
4 – the pale horse (6:7-8)	4 – one third of sun, moon, and stars are darkened (8:12-13)	4 – poured out on the sun (16:8-9)
5 – souls under the altar (6:9-10)	5 – a star falls to the earth (9:1-12)	5 – poured out on the throne of the beast (16:10-11)
6 – a great earthquake (6:12-17)	6 – release of four angels bound at Euphrates (9:13-21)	6 – poured out on the Euphrates River (16:12-14)
School Circle – words of comfort to the 144,000 (7:1-17)	*School Circle* – A Mighty Angel urges perseverance (10:1-11)	*School Circle* – a call to vigilance (16:15-16)
7 – a fire-filled censer hurled to the earth (8:1-15)	7 – loud voices in heaven (11:15-?)	7 – poured out into the air (16:17-?)

Repeat, repeat, and repeat ... this is the best way to learn. The Book of Revelation teaches us that there is only one war, the one being waged for the hearts and minds of people made in the image of the Great King. There is only one General, the man Christ Jesus, unique among the religious leaders of our world, who alone can bring victory to the human race; and there is only one end to the warfare in which we are involved, one which will come quickly, at an hour that no one knows (Matt. 24:36). The strife will end according to the time and in the manner our King chooses. The three cycles of seven judgments in Revelation describe the war in which we are involved, and hint at how it will come to an end. In each of the cycles, Christ speaks to His people. And more than that, He speaks to us daily, promising never to leave us or forsake us (Heb. 13:5). Sometimes He offers words of comfort, reminding us that a day is coming when the war will be over. On other occasions, He reminds us that we are still in the thick of things.

In the "school circle," held between bowl judgments six and seven, our General exhorts us to stay awake: Be vigilant! *"You do not know on what day your Lord will come"* (Matt. 24:42). When the Day of the Lord arrives, you do not want to be found asleep at your post. Servants of the Great King should live every day as if it were their last. The warnings extended to the church in Sardis certainly apply here.

If anyone is to be killed (13:9-10)/Blessed are the dead (14:12-13)

In chapter six, we will evaluate the intelligence assessment that was submitted to the Commander of Troops. Most of this unfolds in Revelation chapters 11-14. As we shall see, the description of enemy forces is terrifying: *"an enormous red dragon"* whose *"tail swept a third of the stars out of the sky"* (12:3-4), *"a beast coming out of the sea"* who *"was given power to make war against the saints and to conquer them"* (13:1, 7), and *"another beast coming out of the earth"* who was able to cause *"fire to come down from heaven ... in full view of men"* (13:11, 13). Anyone listening to this assessment (i.e. readers or hearers of the Apocalypse) might be overcome with despair, but much in the same way as our General offers words of comfort and encouragement in the midst of battle (the three cycles of seven judgments), He now pauses to remind us that, ultimately, the enemy is powerless.

In the war for human souls, Christians are never to pick up the sword.[90] Those who come to Christ must do so freely. Our missionary/evangelistic efforts must be honest, above board, and non-manipulative. Even so, they will meet with great resistance, because the claims of our General are so radical that they challenge

---

[90]The use of the sword is reserved for the State, and it is never to be unsheathed for the purposes of propagating religion. Many Christians, however, as citizens in the kingdom of man, sense a calling to serve in government as part of *"the authority ... God has instituted ... to bring punishment"* upon those who do evil (Rom. 13:2-4). In that capacity, there may be situations when believers in Jesus Christ are called upon to use the sword.

the world and life views of all who do not follow. The only true peace with God is one that comes through faith in Jesus Christ. Many do not want to hear that message, and will offer strong resistance, sometimes to the point of physical violence. This is what Jesus meant when he said:

> *Do not suppose that I have come to bring peace to the earth. I did not come to bring peace, but a sword* (He speaks metaphorically). *For I have come to turn "'a man against his father, a daughter against her mother, a daughter-in-law against her mother-in-law – a man's enemies will be the members of his own household'..."* (Matt. 10:21; cf. Matt. 5:11-12; John 7:7; 1 John 3:13).

In the face of violence, the Christian may be tempted to respond in kind, but that is not part of the battle plan. We are to wait patiently for the justice our King will bring, and if necessary, suffer for Him (14:12). "*If anyone is to go into captivity, into captivity he will go. If anyone is to be killed with the sword, with the sword he will be killed*" (13:10).

And we are not afraid of death (it's the dying part that is difficult!), for death was destroyed at the cross. This is why the Spirit of God cries out, "*Blessed are the dead who die in the Lord ... they will rest from their labor*" (14:13). Our General holds "*the keys of death and Hades*" (1:18), and by trusting Him, we no longer fear these enemies. Physical death means an end to soldiering. The Apostle Paul recognized this when he wrote: "*I desire to depart and be with Christ, which is better by far; but it is more necessary for you that I remain in the body*" (Phil. 1:23-24; cf. 2 Cor. 5:8).

In war, we often memorialize those who die in battle: *"Greater love has no one than this, that one lay down his life for his friends"* (John 15:13). When a soldier throws himself on a grenade, sparing the lives of those in his platoon, the supreme sacrifice is remembered and honored. Often the way in which surviving platoon members live the rest of their lives is dramatically changed. Many Christians also have made the ultimate sacrifice, and the Church is saddened by their deaths; but our text reminds us *"their deeds will follow them"* (14:13). All Saints' Day, November 1, has traditionally been a time when the Church remembers the testimonies of those who have gone on to glory. We remember their noble deeds and are inspired by them; but we also have great hope, knowing that a resurrection follows their physical deaths and ours (20:4, 12). Not one enemy salvo should cause us to fear.

Song of Moses/Song of the Lamb (15:1-8)

> From the Halls of Montezuma
> To the Shores of Tripoli,
> We fight our country's battles
> In the air, on land, and sea.
> First to fight for right and freedom,
> And to keep our honor clean,
> We are proud to claim the title
> Of United States Marine[91]

The *Marines' Hymn* recalls the glory of previous conflicts in which Marines fought and died for their nation, and serves as a reminder of the courage, honor, and commitment expected from those who currently wear the uniform. Played or sung at almost every formal government ceremony, all Marines, whether retired or on active duty, stand at attention when they hear the sound of its opening stanza.

---

[91]Kenneth W. Estes, *The Marine Officer's Guide* Sixth Edition (Annapolis, MD: Naval Institute Press, 1996), 461. Fourth printing, updated in March 2000.

Immediately prior to the last cycle of judgments, "*last, because with them God's wrath is completed*" (v. 1), we find one more "school circle." It involves music, and retired warriors "*standing beside the sea*" (v. 2). Those "*who had been victorious over the beast and his image and over the number of his name ... held harps ... and sang the song of Moses ... and the song of the Lamb*" (vv. 2-3).

Only those who have served in the Great King's Army, the Israel of God (n. Gal. 6:16), are able to sing these songs. Following an ancient victory over the armies of Pharaoh, Miriam and the Israelites began to sing, dance, and play the tambourine:

> *I will sing to the LORD, for he is highly exalted. The horse and its rider he has hurled into the sea. The LORD is my strength and my son; he has become my salvation* (Exod. 15:1-2; cf. Deut. 32).

The Israelites were filled with great joy over the glory and power of God that had been manifested. But the song they sang was a mere foretaste of something far greater. In these verses, the warriors of the Great King sing the song of the *Lamb*, a second Moses, infinitely greater than he of Exodus fame. Those who sing constitute a greater Israel, made up of every tribe and nation, and they celebrate the coming destruction of an Egypt far more nefarious, one ruled by the dragon and his wicked cohorts.[92]

Heaven involves much more than playing harp music for eternity. The songs of victory captured in these few verses will be far more exiting than the greatest Super Bowl ever played; they are infinitely more joyful than the most heart-stirring of concerts. When we stand before this sea of glass, every wrong will be made right, every injustice will be corrected, and every falsehood made true.

---

[92]Although John does not refer to Rev. 19:1-8 as a "song," it is of interest that George Friedrich Handel found his inspiration for the "Hallelujah Chorus" from these verses. The text tells of a great multitude in heaven rejoicing over the destruction of Mystery Babylon. After Handel finished writing the Hallelujah Chorus (he wrote the entire oratorio, *Messiah*, in 24 days) his servant discovered him with tears in his eyes exclaiming "I think I did see all Heaven before me and the great God Himself." Available from http://www.geocities.com/Heartland/Fields/8616/christmas/handel.html; Internet.

All of God's Army will come together in one place, replete with glory. As a people completely redeemed and restored to the true image of our King, we will enjoy Him forever.

an angel ... bound him for a thousand years ... (20:1-6)
The first six verses of chapter twenty may be the most controversial of the Apocalypse. In our introduction, we spoke of "predictive," "historical," and "idealist" approaches to the text. Each of these is based on how the interpreter understands the term "a thousand years." Those who look at the Book of Revelation from a predictive perspective are generally "*pre-millennialists*."[93] They believe that Jesus will return *before* the thousand years of Revelation chapter twenty and set up a political kingdom. Until then, the world will get progressively worse; but at an unknown hour, an angel will come down from heaven, seize the devil, and bind him in the Abyss. At that time, the physical reign of Christ will begin upon the earth, and He will rule for one thousand literal years.

Those who adhere to the historical approach are generally "*post-millennialists*." They believe that Jesus will return *after* the thousand years of Revelation chapter twenty, and that most of the events described in the Book of Revelation were fulfilled during John's lifetime. The Church, bearing the life-transforming message of Jesus Christ, will bring in the kingdom of God. Knowledge will increase, new discoveries will be made, and man's ability to exercise dominion over nature will continue to grow. The powers of evil and darkness will be driven back, the world will be Christianized, and then Jesus will return. For the post-millennialist, the term "a thousand years" is to be understood symbolically. Christ's return will be sudden, and could happen at any time.

---

[93]Within pre-millennialism, there are two basic divisions: 1) Historical premillennialism, and 2) Dispensational premillennialism. Both expect a literal thousand-year reign of Christ upon the earth. Dispensationalism adds such concepts as the rapture of the Church, and seven years of tribulation for those who are left behind.

Christians who look at the Book of Revelation from an idealist perspective are generally "*a-millennialists*." They believe that we are currently living *in* the thousand years of Revelation chapter twenty.[94] Satan is bound, the nations are no longer deceived, and Christ is already reigning in the hearts of believers, and among those who have gone on to glory. At an unknown hour, this spiritual millennium will be over. Satan will be unleashed and judged, and Christ will physically return to the earth. Like the postmillennialist, the expression "a thousand years" is taken symbolically. The reader, to be sure, can learn from all three schools of thought. See Appendix B for further more insight concerning these views.

The stance of this author falls generally within the amillennial/postmillennial camps of interpretation, and for this reason the discussion on millennialism fits well in the chapter entitled "School Circle." Although we are still in the midst of battle, Satan is bound in the Abyss; the cross has sealed his fate (n. Matt. 12:29; John 12:31-32; Col. 2:15), and the nations are no longer deceived – servants of the Most High populate every country on the face of the earth. John brings comfort to the people of God by telling the story of how one of our King's greatest warriors, *an angel coming down out of heaven* (v. 1), *seized the dragon ... and bound him for a thousand years* (v. 2). The ancient serpent and many of his henchmen are locked up (n. 9:1-6; 11:7); the key is thrown away. Even though the dragon's influence is still great,[95] we need not fear him. By way of contrast, our General is alive and well; the host of heaven obeys His every command, and His allies upon the earth are numerous.

School Circle: Concluding reflections
In the midst of an ongoing war, our General speaks to us: Between the sixth and the seventh seals (Rev. 7), He tells us that that we will be protected from the wrath to come. We will make it through

---

[94]Jay Adams, *The Time is at Hand* (Nutley, New Jersey: Presbyterian and Reformed Publishing Company, 1977), 9, refers to this position as "realized millennialism."
[95]Charles Howard Giblin, S.J., *The Book of Revelation: The Open Book of Prophecy* (Collegeville, Minnesota: The Liturgical Press, 1991), 188, points out, "Satan himself attempted to attack the rest of the woman's children (12:17), but was apparently frustrated, standing on the sandy shore of the sea. He was reduced to working through his surrogates, the beasts."

great tribulation and will, one day, drink from *"springs of living water"* (7:17). Between the sixth and seventh trumpets (Rev. 10), He reminds us of our responsibilities to continue sharing the message of the kingdom of God, faithfully bringing it to bear upon the kingdoms of this world. Between the sixth and seventh bowls (16:15), He exhorts us to remain vigilant. We do not know when the Lord will come, and should live every day as if it were our last. In the middle of a very sobering intelligence assessment (13:10; 14:13), our Commander reminds us that not even death should deter us from our mission. When persecuted for our faith, there is no need to respond violently. If we happen to lose our lives in the midst of combat, we will rest from our labor, and the days of our soldiering will be over. Prior to the last cycle of judgments (15:1-8), we sing the song of Moses and the song of the Lamb, joining in with other warriors who went before us. Finally, in Revelation chapter twenty, our General informs us that Satan, the enemy general, is already imprisoned, chained in the Abyss; He reminds us that our Army is very large, with allies all around the world. It is only a matter of time before the last trumpet shall sound, and Day of the Lord will bring about an end to the world as we know it now. An intelligence assessment is in order prior to the outbreak of final hostilities, and that is precisely what follows in chapter six.

Chapter 6

INTELLIGENCE ASSESSMENT
(Revelation 11:1-6; 12; 13:1-8, 11-18; 14:1-5; 17; 19:11-16)

> *Or suppose a king is about to go to war against another king. Will he not first sit down and consider whether he is able with ten thousand men to oppose the one coming against him with twenty thousand?*
>   - Luke 14:31

I will give power to my two witnesses (11:1-6)
The U.S. Department of Defense Dictionary of Military and Associated Words (2003) defines military intelligence as: 1) "The product resulting from the collection, processing, integration, analysis, evaluation, and interpretation of available information concerning foreign countries or areas," and 2) "Information and knowledge about an adversary obtained through observation, investigation, analysis, or understanding."[96] In addition, commanders do a serious assessment of their own strength levels long before any engagement with enemy forces takes place.

    In the eleventh chapter of Revelation, John continues to participate in the heavenly drama. The voice that he *"had heard from heaven"* (10:8) now commands him to *"measure the temple of God ... and count the worshipers there"* (v. 1), but he is to *"exclude the outer court ... because it has been given over to the Gentiles"* (v. 2; cf.

---
[96]Available from http://www.answers.com/topic/intelligence; Internet.

Luke 21:24). ("Gentiles" in this case refers to those who reject Christ; it does not mean "non-Jewish," n. 1 Cor. 12:2, KJV; Eph. 2:11). Our King, it seems, is asking for a census. "Just how many are in my Army, John? ... and by the way, make sure you don't count those bad guys who are trampling on the holy city; they belong to the enemy." Before John is able to come back with an answer, the narrative spins off in another direction, and we never hear the results of what God has requested – or so it appears.

Surely, the Most High knows exactly how many are in His Army. Perhaps His request was rhetorical, and in verse three He begins to answer: *"I will give power to my two witnesses, and they will prophesy for 1,260 days."* The two witnesses – and Jewish law requires the testimony of two men in order to be valid (n. Deut. 17:6; John 8:17) – are identified as *"the two olive trees and the two lampstands that stand before the Lord of the earth"* (v. 4; cf. Zech. 4:1-14). Their powers include the ability to devour their enemies with fire (v. 5), *"to shut up the sky so that it will not rain,"* *"to turn the waters into blood,"* and to *"strike the earth with every kind of plague"* (v. 6).

Many futurists believe that the two witnesses are Moses and Elijah. These are to participate in a ministry that will last for three and one half years. Most suggest that their work will take place during the second half of the seven-year tribulation period, a time known as "The Great Tribulation."[97] The choice is intriguing. The Old Testament indicates that both Moses and Elijah would return before the end of the age (Deut. 18:18; Mal. 4:5). Jews living at the time of Christ clearly expected this to happen (Matt. 16:14; 27:47; Mark. 6:15; John 1:21; 6:14; 7:40). God used the ministries of Moses and Elijah in powerful ways: they turned water into blood (Exod. 7:20), struck the earth with plagues (Exod. 8:2ff), devoured their enemies with fire (2 Kings 1:10), and stopped the rain from falling (1 Kings 17:1). Mystery surrounded their final days: Elijah rode off into the heavens in a chariot of fire (2 Kings 2:11); and

---

[97]Clarence Larkin, *The Book of Revelation*, Glenside, PA: Rev. Clarence Larkin Estate, 1919, 84, and John Walvoord, *The Bible Knowledge Commentary, New Testament* (Wheaton, Illinois: Victor Books, 1986), 955. Wiersbe, 89, however, places this 1,260-day period in the first half of the tribulation.
Note, also, remarks contained in footnote 48.

although Moses died a normal death (Deut. 34:5), the Book of Jude informs us that Michael the archangel disputed with the devil over his body (v. 9). One of the issues with which the futurists must grapple, however, is the theological position that Moses and Elijah have already come.[98]

There may be something else at play in this text. If our King is responding to His own rhetorical question, "Just how many are in my Army, John," perhaps what seems to be a digression is not that at all. When He says *"I will give power to my two witnesses"* (v. 3), the question is answered. The explanatory comment, *"these are the two olive trees and the two lampstands"* (v. 4; cf. Zech. 4:1-14), provides further insight.

In the Old Testament, the nation of Israel is referred to as an olive tree (Jer. 11:16; Hos. 14:6); in the New, the metaphor continues: Israel remains an olive tree, but some of the original branches have been broken off because of unbelief. Gentiles, who place their faith in Jesus Christ, are grafted in (Rom. 11:17-24; cf. Eph. 2:11-14). In the Old Testament, Israel is *"a light for the Gentiles"* (Isa. 42:6; cf. Isa. 10:17). In the New, those who follow Jesus Christ are *"the light of the world"* (Matt. 5:14). Eller believes the image points to both Jewish and Gentile Christians and serves as "a plea for ecumenicity and the *fullness* of God's church."[99] In the same way that John used the expression *"144,000 from all the tribes of Israel"* (7:4) as a symbol for the Church, he now uses the imagery of olive trees, lampstands (1:20), and two witnesses to portray the mighty human element in the Army of the Lord of hosts.

---

[98] In speaking about John the Baptist, Jesus said, *"if you are willing to accept it, he is the Elijah who was to come. He who has ears, let him hear"* (Mt. 11:14-15; cf. Mt. 17:12). Both Moses and Elijah appeared to Peter, James and John on the Mount of Transfiguration (Mt. 17:3).

[99] Eller, *The Most Revealing Book*, 116, states: "The church of John's day was rather conspicuously divided into congregations of Christians, one group having come out of a Jewish background and the other out of a Gentile background. Although holding a common faith and worshipping a common Lord, their whole style and way of doing things undoubtedly was quite diverse ... it may well be that John is using the twoness of these figures to say that the mission of the church wants and needs the witness of both the Jewish and the Gentile Christians."

In the great battle being waged against the beasts that rise out of earth and sea, the Church marches towards a Holy City upon whose foundations *"the names of the twelve apostles of the Lamb"* (21:14) are written, and upon whose gates *"the names of the twelve tribes of Israel"* (21:12) are inscribed. The mission of these two witnesses includes an invitation for others to join in. As Christians, we rejoice to participate in this mighty Army, and need not fear any of the weapons in the arsenal of the enemy.

God's Church is able to call fire down from heaven and strike the earth with plagues. Moses and the great prophets of the Old Testament did such things, as did Jesus and the Apostles of the New. The two witnesses perform these kinds of miracles in order to point people to the great King of Heaven. During His earthly ministry our General told His foot soldiers: *"I tell you the truth, anyone who has faith in me will do what I have been doing. He will do even greater things than these"* (John 14:12). He tells us that even *"the gates of Hades"* will not prevail (Matt. 16:18). As we look down the strands of time, there is great truth to His words. Empires have risen and fallen, wars have been waged, and all sorts of natural and man-made disasters have afflicted the earth. The Church, however, is alive and well, and Her influence is great. The two witnesses still walk the earth.

a woman clothed with the sun ... (12:1-17)

In Revelation chapter twelve, we encounter several of the combatants involved in the ongoing spiritual war. The first is a pregnant woman, *"clothed with the sun, with the moon under her feet and a crown of twelve stars on her head"* (vv. 1-2). She gave birth to a male child who is to *"rule all the nations with an iron scepter"* and who, later, is *"snatched up to God and to his throne"* (v. 5). The woman then flees into the wilderness where God protects her from the dragon for 1,260 days (we will discuss the significance of this number in chapter seven).

There are many who believe that this woman is the Virgin Mary, and on the surface, the choice seems quite plausible. Mary gave birth to a son who rules the nations and ascended to heaven, but there is no record, either in Scripture or in secular history, of her fleeing to the desert for 1, 260 days. The woman is a symbol of something far greater. She is the human community out of which Christ came. The sun, moon, and stars that clothe her point us to Joseph's dream (Gen. 37:9), and to the house of Israel, the great nation from whom "*is traced the human ancestry of Christ*" (Ro. 9:5). In addition to the male child, her offspring also includes "*those who obey God's commandments and hold to the testimony of Jesus*" (12:17). The woman clothed with the sun – like the two witnesses in the previous section, and the 144,000 from all the tribes of Israel (pp. 101-104, above) – is a symbol for the Church of Jesus Christ, placed upon this earth to bear witness to the Most High. Although still in the wilderness, she is protected by God (vv. 6, 14-16) and has overcome the devil by "*the blood of the Lamb*" (v. 11).

an enormous red dragon ... (12:3-17)
Also in Revelation 12, we are given our first glimpse of the enemy general. He has "*seven heads and ten horns and seven crowns on his heads.*[100] *His tail swept a third of the stars out of the sky and flung them to the earth*" (vv. 3-4). He sought to devour the male child (v. 5), but in failing, "*went off to make war against ... those who obey God's commandments*" (v. 17). Ultimately, he is left standing on the shore of the sea (13:1), watching as his minions engage in combat. This is one of the few instances in the Book of Revelation where a symbol is defined for us. Most of the time we are left to our own devices, crying out to God for wisdom (13:18). Verse nine tells us that the red dragon is "*called the devil or Satan, who leads the whole world astray.*"

Nonetheless, we need great wisdom as we try to understand this passage. It seems as if the host of heaven (angels) has been around a lot longer than God's human army, and it is also apparent that there was a great rebellion. Satan sought to usurp the throne of our King. A "*war in heaven*" ensued, and "*Michael and his angels fought against the dragon*" (v. 7), ultimately hurling him "*to the earth, and his angels with him*" (v. 9; Isa. 14:11-15; Ezek. 28:12-19;

---
[100]See pp. 125-127 for a possible interpretation of these numbers.

Dan. 8:5-10; Luke 10:18). One third of the angels followed the lead of our nemesis and joined him in rebellion and banishment. Terrible acts of aggression were about to take place against the earth and its inhabitants. *"Woe to the earth and the sea,"* the text tells us, *"because the devil has gone down to you!"* (v. 12).

Human beings first encountered the serpent in the Garden of Eden (Gen. 3:1).[101] His threatening presence in Paradise challenged the authority of our King, and brought about the fall of the human race. Adam, who was entrusted with defending the Garden, and with protecting it from evil (Gen. 2:15),[102] failed in his mission. As a result, he and his wife were banished from the Garden, and *"forced to work the ground"* from which they were taken (Gen. 3:23). But God was not through. Human beings were created in His image; they were to *"rule over the fish of the sea and the birds of the air and over every living creature that moves on the ground"* (Gen. 1:28). Our King was very pleased with His creation, and He was not about to allow the dragon to have such an easy victory. In response to the evil that now permeated Paradise, and in order to restore the common good, God was about to launch a military operation of unprecedented scale. In His wrath, He cursed the serpent and told him, *"I will put enmity between you and the woman, and between your offspring and hers; he will crush your head, and you will strike his heel"* (Gen. 3:15). The reference was to our General, One who would be born of a woman, and groomed to lead the Armies of God.

Because of this, the devil was *"filled with fury"* (v. 12). He *"stood in front of the woman who was about to give birth, so that he might devour her child the moment it was born"* (v. 4). The Child, however, was born, and His teachings forever changed our world; but He ended up on a cross, and when He died, the dragon and his legions of demons surely rejoiced. Their laughter must have reached

---

[101] Traditional understanding connects the red dragon of Revelation with the serpent in Genesis.
[102] Marine Battle Skills Training Handbook: Book 1, PVT-CAPT, General Military Subjects With User's Guide (Arlington, VA: Marine Corps Institute, August 1995), 1-9-4, General order #1 for the Marine Corps, "To take charge of this post and all government property in view," captures the essence of the Hebrew term "Shamir," translated as "take care" in Gen. 2:15.

up to the heavens; the "child" was finally devoured. But God had the last laugh; on the third day, the "seed of the woman" had risen from the dead. The mortal wound was a mere "strike at His heel." Soon, the serpent's head would be crushed. The devil knows that he is a defeated enemy, and *"that his time is short"* (v. 12). *"Enraged at the woman ... (he) went off to make war against the rest of her offspring – those who obey God's commandments and hold to the testimony of Jesus"* (v. 17). This war, ladies and gentlemen, is against us, and it is against everything that is good and holy. The cross, however, has limited the powers of the dragon. As our General has already reminded us, Satan is bound in the Abyss.[103] He can only stand on the shore and watch (13:1), as others take his place on the battlefield. We who serve in Christ's Army have already achieved victory *"by the blood of the Lamb"* (v. 11). The prophecy of Genesis 3:15 was fulfilled at the cross.

a male child, who will rule all the nations ... (12:5-17)
There is very little doubt as to the identity of this combatant. As the great Christmas hymn declares:

> This, this is Christ the King,
> Whom shepherds guard and angels sing:
> Haste, haste to bring him laud,
> The Babe, the Son of Mary.[104]

Christians believe that Isaiah the prophet (9:6-7) as well as the Psalmist (2:7-9; cf. Rev. 2:27; 19:15) predicted the coming of a child who would rule the nations. This text mentions only His birth and ascension – He was *"snatched up to God and to his throne"* (v. 5; cf. Acts 1:9). In between those two events lies much of our story: His teachings revolutionized the world; His death on the cross paid the penalty for our sins; and His resurrection from the dead dealt the serpent and his followers a fatal blow. Now, Christ is snatched up

---
[103] See comments on pp. 113-114.
[104] "What Child Is This, Who, Laid to Rest" Text: William C. Dix. Music: Traditional English melody. *BOOK OF WORSHIP FOR UNITED STATES FORCES: A collection of Hymns and Worship Resources for Military Personnel of the United States of America* (Washington, DC: U.S. Government Printing Office, 1974), 270.

to the throne. He has taken the War Scroll from the hand of our King, and is currently waging the campaign that will rid our world of evil forever.

And I saw a beast coming out of the sea ... (13:1-8)
As the dragon *"stood on the shore"* (v. 1), a beast, having ten horns, seven heads, with crowns on each of the horns, rose up out of the sea. It looked like a leopard, but had feet like a bear and a mouth like a lion. The dragon gave this beast its power. As the text continues, we are told, *"one of the heads of the beast seemed to have had a fatal wound, but the fatal wound had been healed"* (v. 3). As a result, the world worshipped the beast, as well as the dragon who gave him power, and asked, *"Who is like the beast? Who can make war against him?"* (v. 4).

Some commentators believe this beast to be the Antichrist, a man possessed by the devil (n. John 13:2), who will take his place on the world stage during the Great Tribulation. Over the years, more than a few names have been suggested as possible candidates. Some of the more notable mentions have included: the Emperors Nero, Caligula, and Domitian of Rome; Mohamed, Martin Luther, Oliver Cromwell, King George III of England, Napoleon Bonaparte, Adolf Hitler, King Juan Carlos of Spain, Ronald Wilson Reagan (with six letters in each of his names), Anwar Sadat, Michael Gorbachev, and various Popes throughout the ages. These kinds of speculations are both dangerous and embarrassing.

The physical description of the sea beast, however, takes us in a totally different direction – away from the concept of an individual and towards the idea of institutional evil. The composite image of this beast – part leopard, part bear, and part lion – points us to Daniel's vision, where *"four great beasts ... came up out of the sea"* (Dan. 7:3). The first was like a lion, the second was like a bear, the third was like a leopard, and the fourth was *"terrifying and frightening and very powerful ... it crushed and devoured its victims ... and it had ten horns"* (Dan. 7:3-7). Daniel was told that these beasts are *"four kingdoms that will rise from the earth,"* and that the fourth one was particularly dreadful. It was to *"devour the whole earth, trampling it down and crushing it."* Furthermore, *"the ten horns are ten kings who will come from this kingdom"* (Dan. 7:17, 23-24).

It may be that the very first readers of the Book of Revelation were familiar with Daniel's prophecies, and for them, the dreadful beast that rose up out of the sea pointed to the Roman Empire. This "beast" was more evil than the empires of Babylon (the lion), Persia (the bear), and Greece (the leopard) combined. The ancient historian Pliny (c. A.D. 61-112), records some of Rome's atrocities against early believers:

> Those accused of being Christians were asked before the governor, as judge, whether the accusation was true. Anyone who denied it had to substantiate the denial by a ritual sacrifice before statues of the gods and the image of the emperor and curse Christ. Anyone who admitted being a Christian was asked a second and third time with the threat of the death penalty. Those who persisted were condemned.[105]

To the early readers of the Apocalypse, Rome was responsible for *"the souls of those who had been slain because of the word of God and the testimony they had maintained"* (6:9; 20:4). The Empire was the dreadful harlot who is *"drunk with the blood of the saints"* (17:6), while those who *"had not worshiped the beast or his image and had not received his mark on their foreheads or their hands"* (20:4) referred to those who refused to participate in the "Roman cult of the state and the emperor".[106] The ten horns of our text may well refer to the first ten of Rome's Emperors, but interpreters are at wit's end in attempting to identify them.[107] Many feel that Nero

---

[105] Klaus Wengst, *Pax Romana and the Peace of Jesus Christ* (Fortress Press, 1987), 120.
[106] Ibid.
[107] Smith, 68, says, "Those ten rulers are either a succession of ten Roman emperors, or they are ten puppet kings allied to the Romans. Either way, in John's view the Roman Empire as a massive system of political and economic power was the instrument of Satan and posed a severe threat to the existence of the church as a community of faith."

may be the head which *"seemed to have had a fatal wound, but ... had been healed"* (v. 3).[108] Like apocryphal stories of Hitler being alive in our day, following the accounts of his suicide, those about Nero, who also took his own life, persisted in his.

But there is something far more important going on; the world did not come to an end when the Roman Empire fell, yet Christians throughout the ages – especially those trapped in totalitarian regimes – have been greatly comforted by the words of the Apocalypse. This beast, and the numbers "seven" and "ten" used to describe it, may symbolize something far more insidious than the Roman Empire. It is a *system* of evil, spiritual in nature, which constantly rears its ugly head, seeking to usurp for itself the worship that belongs to the true and the living God. The sea beast is human government gone wrong. Something that God created for the welfare and benefit of His children, twisted and perverted. There is a dualism, a struggle between good and evil, inherent in the Book of Revelation, and we must be very careful where lines are drawn. No human government is free of sin: the dualism, the struggle between good government and bad, exists within every nation. No nation can ever say, "God is on our side," while the other was for Satan. The sea beast is alive and well *anytime* that *any* nation ignores justice and human rights. As Christians, we have a loyalty that runs far deeper than that due our homeland. It is never "my country, right or wrong." For these reasons, Christians are often suspect; we are called to resist the sea beast anytime he rears his ugly head.

Having said all this, there are times when the sea beast appears to sit squarely upon a political throne. He seemed to be very powerful in Egypt during the time of Pharoah, in Babylon when Nebuchadnezzar was king, and in Rome under the early Emperors. He was the sinister presence behind Nazi Germany and the

---

[108]Walter E. Pilgrim, *Uneasy Neighbors: Church and State in the New Testament* (Fortress Press, 1999), 152, writes, "This oft-repeated reference originates in a rumor that swept over the Roman empire after Nero's suicide in 68 C.E., a rumor that Nero had not really died and that he was about to revenge his death by returning at the head of the Parthian armies, Rome's feared enemies to the East."

old Soviet Union, having usurped the worship that belongs only to God, while persecuting those who would not bow down. This beast often promises peace, safety, and security, but as soon as he has you in his wicked grasp, bondage and oppression pull you to your knees. Time and again, it seems as if this beast has been slain, but he always rises again in some other sinister form.[109] Like his master, the sea beast opposes the God of the Bible. In the Old Testament, he sought to crush the nation of Israel. In our era he seeks to marginalize or eradicate the Church.

Both the dragon and the sea beast have seven heads and ten horns; both are perfectly evil in their knowledge and authority. The sea beast is made in the image of his master, but he is not identical. The dragon had crowns on each of his heads, while the sea beast had crowns on his horns. (The chart below offers a concise summary.) Mounce suggests that the shift from "heads" to "horns" indicate the brute force often used by repressive regimes to keep people under control.[110]

Scripture reference	Description	Number of Heads	Number of Horns	Number of Crowns
Rev. 12:3	Red Dragon	7	10	7 (on heads)
Rev. 13:1	Sea Beast	7	10	10 (on horns)
Rev. 13:11	Earth Beast	-	2	-
Rev. 17:3	Scarlet Beast	7	10	-
Dan. 7:7	Fourth Beast	-	10	-

The earliest Christians may have remembered Daniel's description of the end state of the dreadful beast that appeared in his vision: *"the court will sit, and his power will be taken away and completely destroyed forever. Then the sovereignty, power and greatness of the kingdoms under the whole heaven will be handed over to the saints, the people of the Most High"* (Dan. 7:26-27). The Book of Revela-

---

[109]The reader will note that the beast itself did not suffer a fatal wound, only one of its many heads (v. 3).
[110]Mounce, 250.

tion tells us that the sea beast will be *"thrown alive into the fiery lake of burning sulfur"* (19:20). As Christians, we do not fear him; we live in hope. We bear witness to him,[111] yet resist him with all of our might (nonviolently) when he opposes our God (n. Acts 5:29), patiently waiting for the Day when our General brings about his demise. To answer the question: *"who can make war against him?"* (v. 4), we might suggest to those prone to worship this idol, that there is One who does. He already reigns in the heavens. By serving in His Army, we will never be helpless in the face of human government, regardless of how wicked it might be. In the meantime, we occupy the territory God has given, serving as salt and light in a world often dominated by this beast's unsavory and dark ideologies.

another beast, coming out of the earth ... (13:11-18)

An assessment of yet another enemy combatant occurs in chapter thirteen: a beast rising out of the earth who had *"two horns like a lamb, but ... spoke like a dragon* (v. 11). Like the sea beast, the earth beast also has great authority, able to perform *"miraculous signs, even causing fire to come down from heaven"* (v. 13). He uses his power to make the inhabitants of the earth *"worship the first beast, whose fatal head wound had been healed"* (v. 12). Ultimately, he deceives the earth people, forcing everyone *"small and great, rich and poor, free and slave, to receive a mark on his right hand or on his forehead"* (v. 16). Without this mark, *"which is the name of the beast or the number of his name,"* no one could *"buy or sell"* (v. 17).

The earth beast is a symbol of religion gone wrong.[112] Rather than use his great power (although with two horns he has less power than the sea beast) to point people into a relationship with the true and the living God, this creature perverts ultimate loyalties. His desire is to deceive humanity into worshiping the sea beast. For this he uses his great powers of oratory, for he is able to speak like a dragon (v. 11). The earth beast is the one who caused the Egyptian people to worship Pharaoh, crushing those who would not

---

[111]See footnote 79.

[112]The earth beast is not a symbol for any particular religious tradition; he is a symbol for the evil that is possible in any religion.

comply, forcing them as slaves to make bricks without straw (Ex. 5:11). He was the influence behind Caesar worship in Rome and the "The Thousand Year Reich" in Nazi Germany, slave states separated by 1900 years, both of which called for the death of those who would not bow down. He deceived the good people of the Soviet Union, and of those living in communist regimes all over the world, causing them to look to the State as the wellspring of spiritual needs. He has frequently reared up his ugly head in the Western World, pretending to "civilize the savage" while enslaving him, stealing his land, or destroying his economy. The earth beast is alive and well; he is the god of "isms." If he is able to channel our ultimate loyalties into socialism, capitalism (and neither of these are necessarily wrong), hedonism, stoicism, or relativism, he has succeeded in his mission. Citizens of oppressive regimes that tout one these "isms" will not be able to hold down good jobs if they fail to embrace it. If faith in God can be replaced by an "ism," the earth beast has arrived. Any State that tells its citizenry how to worship is, indeed, a dangerous beast. As servants of the Great King, we are called to separate ourselves from him (2 Cor. 6:17; Rev. 18:4).

The mark he attempts to place on everyone's right hand or forehead may have some connection with the phylacteries[113] worn by the Israelites in the Old Testament and by Orthodox Jews today. For the Jew, the phylactery is a sign of total devotion to God. The earth beast perverts this; he wants to steer this worship away from the Most High, and towards the sea beast. If we do not cooperate, there will be economic consequences.

Implicitly we are warned not to take *"the number of the beast, for it is man's number. His number is 666"* (v.18). No one is absolutely certain as to the meaning of this passage, and in the Greek text, numbers are not even used. The ancient Greeks had no nu-

---

[113]Phylacteries consist of two small square cases of leather, one of which is worn on the forehead, the other on the upper left arm. The case for the forehead holds four distinct compartments, that for the arm only one. They contain narrow strips of parchment on which are copied passages from the Pentateuch, viz., Exodus 13:1-10; and Deuteronomy 6:4-9; 11:13-21. *Catholic Encyclopedia*: Phylacteries. Available from www.newadvent.org/org/cathen/12046a.htm; Internet.

merals; letters of the alphabet were used for counting purposes. Morris tells us "the first nine letters of the alphabet were used for the units, the next for the tens, and so on."[114] As a result, some ancient words had a "mystical numerology." 'The Greek word "abrasax,"' for example, 'whose letters add up to 365, the number of the days of the year, was thought to be a powerful magical charm.'[115] "666" may have been just such a word, and many scholars feel that it was a reference to the Emperor Nero, "*the name of the beast*" (v. 17). Others suggest Caligula, Domitian, the Caesars in general, or the Roman Empire as a whole.[116] The warning in this passage, then, would be for Christians to avoid becoming too closely affiliated with the Imperial regime. Samuel Johnson, the great English author, once wrote, "Patriotism is the last refuge of a scoundrel."[117] There is a loyalty demanded of the Christian that runs higher than that owed to the State (n. 2 Ti. 2:4). The voice of any religion that preaches blind, unquestioning obedience to one's political leaders originates from this hideous seven-headed creature that rises out of the earth.

Another school of thought is that "666" is "mystical numerology" that refers to "*man's number*" (v. 18). Morris points out that, "if we take the sum of the values represented by the letters of the … Greek name 'Jesus', it comes to 888. Each digit is one more than seven, the perfect number. But 666 yields the opposite phenomenon, for each digit falls short." The warning then becomes, "we must rely on God rather than upon ourselves." "Unregenerate man is persistently evil. He bears the mark of the beast in all he does. Civilization without Christ is necessarily under the dominion of the evil one."[118]

---

[114]Morris, 174.
[115]Rist, 86.
[116]Wilcock, 128.
[117]James Boswell, *Life of Johnson*, (1970), 615; available from http://www.bartleby.com/73/1306.html; Internet.
[118]Morris, 174.

Intelligence Assessment

Many Christians are so consumed about looking for a literal "666" in a bar code, upon a microchip, or hidden within e-mail messages that they totally miss the meaning of the passage. Despite difficulties of interpretation, John was not suggesting that the technological advances of our era were to be regarded with suspicion. Although the symbolism may not be completely clear, the text certainly tells us not to rely upon our own strength or upon human government for the source of ultimate meaning. We are to place our trust in the Lamb, who has already bound the dragon, leaving him upon the *"shore of the sea"* (13:1); and we are not to be deceived by either of the dragon's lieutenants (the sea and earth beasts), both of whom battle furiously for the souls of human beings made in the image of our King. We patiently wait for the day when our General returns and throws these beasts *"alive into the fiery lake of burning sulfur"* (19:20). By trusting the Lord God and by following the commands of His Great General, any supposed power represented by the mysterious symbol of "666" will have no influence in our lives.

the Lamb ... and with him 144,000 (14:1-5)
Commanders of troops routinely take formal group pictures of the men and women who serve in their units. Sometimes dress blues or whites are worn, while on other occasions "cammies," pressed and clean, serve as the uniform of the day. Everyone stands at attention, tall and proud. Officers and senior enlisted personnel are in the front ranks; those junior to them line up in the rear. Military hardware, mascots, or other significant symbols may be included in the photograph, and background scenery is carefully selected. By the time a picture is taken, the unit has already gone through hard training or even combat. The men and women in the picture know each other, know the capabilities of the unit, and are proud of their accomplishments. These photographs are displayed in prominent places; they remind warriors of past accomplishments, and serve as a source of inspiration for any future undertakings.

We have encountered the Lamb and the 144,000 on earlier occasions. In this passage, they pose as combat veterans. The Lamb, of course, is our General, in charge of the great campaign waged against Satan and the forces of darkness. The number 144,000 serves as a symbol for the Church,[119] the mighty human element in the Army of our King; the text almost begs the photograph. In the background is Mount Zion (cf. Ps. 2:6; Heb. 12:22). The Father's name is already written on the foreheads of these warriors (in 7:3, the angel was only beginning to accomplish that task), and the contrast with those who received the mark of the beast could not be greater (see Rev. 14:11; 16:2; 19:20). There are sounds of rushing waters in the background, and of *"harpists playing their harps"* (v. 2). The 144,000 sing the words to a cadence that no one else knows; their training and periods of combat have purified them from the cares of the world. *"They follow the Lamb wherever he goes"* (v. 4). There is great pride in this unit, and even though the war is not yet over, no one will be able to stop such a formidable force. Many traditions refer to this group as "the Church triumphant."

---

[119]See comments on pp. 101-103.

Intelligence Assessment

the great prostitute ... sitting on a scarlet beast ... (17:1-18)
The combatants of chapter seventeen also appeared on earlier occasions, but under different names. The woman upon the scarlet beast is none other than the earth beast of Revelation chapter thirteen.[120] (In 16:13 and 19:20, she is also called "the false prophet.") The monster upon which she sits is the dreadful sea beast of 13:1-8, who demands the allegiance of the whole earth.[121] In this chapter, their relationship to each other is even clearer.

The woman is portrayed as a prostitute. The kings of the earth (i.e. the sea beast/scarlet beast) committed adultery with her, and the inhabitants of the earth (those who reject our General and our King) *"were intoxicated with the wine of her adulteries"* (v. 2). She was *"drunk with the blood of the saints"* (v. 6), and is identified as *"the great city that rules over the kings of the earth"* (v. 18). On her forehead were inscribed the words:

MYSTERY
BABYLON THE GREAT
THE MOTHER OF PROSTITUTES
AND OF THE ABOMINATIONS OF THE
EARTH (v. 5).

---

[120]Giblin, 164, believes the great harlot was a caricature of "Roma," the patron goddess of Rome. Ancient coins often picture her as a warrior riding upon a horse-drawn chariot or seated upon seven hills or upon a throne. Several of the seven cities of Revelation had temples dedicated to her. http://www.apocalipsis.org/rev-hist.htm; Internet, mentions Smyrna, Ephesus, and Pergamum.

[121]The descriptions of the scarlet beast and the sea beast are nearly identical. See chart on p. 127.

122

The beast upon which she rides *"had seven heads and ten horns"* (v. 4). The seven heads of this beast *"are seven hills on which the woman sits. They are also seven kings"* (vv. 9-10). The ten horns *"are ten kings who have not yet received a kingdom"* (v. 12). We are told that the beast and the ten horns *"will hate the prostitute. They will bring her to ruin and leave her naked; they will eat her flesh and burn her with fire"* (v. 17).

The seven hills (v. 9) appear to refer to Rome, the center of the great Empire where Caesar was divine and where Christians were persecuted, but the imagery may run deeper. Attempts to identify the seven kings (v. 10) and the ten kings (v. 12) seem futile.[123] Many believe the seven kings refer to the Emperors Augustus, Tiberius, Caligula, Claudius, and Nero. The one who is would be Vespasian, while Titus would be the one yet to come. [In this scenario, Nero would be the *"beast who once was, and now is not, is an eighth king.*

---

[122]David E. Aune, *Revelation 17-22*. WORD Biblical Commentary, vol. 52c. (Nashville: Thomas Nelson Publishers, 1998), .

[123]See comments on pp. 125-127.

He belongs to the seven and is going to his destruction" (v. 11; cf. Dan. 7:7-8). Domitian, widely regarded as a "returned" Nero, wielded imperial power much in the same way as his predecessor.][124]

Others having difficulty with this interpretation have suggested a succession of Empires – Egypt, Ninevah, Babylon, Persia, Greece, Rome, and Constantinople.[125] In keeping with our symbolic principle of interpretation, it could be, as Wilcock suggests, that the "real meaning of the sevenfold King is political power." (Seven in this instance would be a symbol for perfect evil.) "Christians of *any* century," he continues, "have been able to look back over a succession of worldly governments ('five ... have fallen'), have recognized another power in their own time ('one is'), and have normally expected the system to continue at least for a while longer (the seventh yet to come and remain for a little)."[126] The beast that "*once was, now is not, and will come up out of the Abyss* (v. 8) would then refer to the staying power of this scarlet monster.

There is a system of religion, metaphorically referred to as "Mystery Babylon," which has perverted and twisted the worship that belongs to God, almost from the very beginning. This harlot persecutes and oppresses the people of the Most High, and seeks to destroy the souls of men and women made in the image of our King. Wicked human government has always enjoyed her support. She may have made her first appearance when Nimrod, "*a mighty hunter before the LORD*" (Gen. 10:9), established one of the centers of his kingdom in Babylon (hence "Mystery Babylon"). A tower was built in the city in order that the people might "*make a name for themselves*" (Gen. 11:4). The great prostitute later became the influence behind Pharoah worship in Egypt, and behind the exaltation of the Canaanite god Bel. The Babylonian Empire, with its great tower of Bel, later brought about the destruction of Jerusalem and its temple in 587 BC. Mystery Babylon encouraged Emperor worship in ancient Rome; the pillaging of India, Africa, and America by western European powers; the racism of Nazi Ger-

---

[124]Giblin, 165.
[125]Mounce, 314-315.
[126]Wilcock, 164.

many; and the secularism of the Soviet Union. Surely she takes great pleasure today, anytime a third world market is exploited for economic gain by first world powers. Mystery Babylon rides proudly on the back of the scarlet beast, but there is a day coming when she will be brought to ruin. God will put enmity in the heart of the beast upon which she rides, and the beast and his people will "*leave her naked ... eat her flesh and burn her with fire*" (v. 16).

The angel in this text was warning John not to compromise with the religious system of the Roman Empire. The message he passed on to his readers is one that also applies to us: flee this harlot, and resist the beast upon which she rides. Human government has a propensity to "use" religion to further its own agenda; the Church is easily enamored with the trappings of temporal politics. Christians, above all others, are to follow the commands of their General, and not compromise with the agenda of the enemy. Much like a prostitute, false religion can enjoy the baubles of worldly trinkets for a season, but when a new lover comes along, she may no longer be found attractive, and will be quickly abandoned. The great prostitute and the hideous monster upon which she rides are headed for destruction. We are reminded not to fear these enemies.

... a white horse, whose rider is called Faithful and True ... (19:11-16)

The last of the combatants mentioned in our intelligence assessment is the greatest of them all. Heaven was opened for John and he was able to see our General in full regalia. "*His eyes are like blazing fire*" (v. 12), and "*out of his mouth comes a sharp sword with which to strike down the nations*" (v. 15; cf. Isa. 11:4). On his robe are the words "KING OF KINGS AND LORD OF LORDS" (v. 16; cf. Deut. 10:7; Dan. 2:47; 1 Tim. 6:15; Rev. 17:14). The "*robe dipped in blood*" (v. 13; cf. Isa. 63:1-6) suggests the victory already achieved at the cross. "The armies of heaven" (v. 14; cf. 2 Kings 6:16-17; Isa. 13:4; Joel 2:11) are made up of angels clothed with "*fine linen, white and clean*" (n. 15:6). "*With justice* (and this is the only war that is perfectly just) *he judges and makes war*" (v. 11). The Lord Jesus Christ is poised and ready for battle. When the great Day arrives, nothing will stop Him.

Intelligence Assessment

Final analysis

Each of these combatants has been engaged in warfare for a long time. Our King has delegated great authority to the earthly component of His Army. The Church – symbolically referred to as "the two witnesses," "the woman clothed with the sun," or "the 144,000" – has driven back the powers of darkness and has occupied much of the territory formerly under the enemy's control. Two thousand years ago, our General (the Lamb/the male child/the rider on the white horse) inflicted a mortal wound upon the leader of the enemy forces (the red dragon/Satan/the devil), binding him, and taking away much of his power. Satan's lieutenants – the sea beast (the scarlet beast) and the earth beast (the great prostitute/the false prophet) – continue to bring great destruction upon the earth through perverted human government and a religion that worships it. In the next chapter, however, the war comes to an end. Our General, and the *heavenly* component of His Army – the angelic host – will descend from heaven and destroy the Devil, the sea beast, the earth beast, and all who would ally themselves with them, forever ridding our world of their evil influence.

Chapter 7

THE DAY OF THE LORD (ARMAGEDDON)

(Revelation 6:12-17; 8-9; 11-14; 16; 18; 19:17-21; 20:7-10)

> *I know war as few other men now living know it, and nothing to me is more revolting.*[127]
> - General Douglas MacArthur

42 months/1,260 days/time, times and half a time (chap 11-13) The struggle for the soul of humanity has been going on ever since the serpent had his little "chat" with Adam and Eve. At the cross, our General achieved a strategic victory, and we who align ourselves with Him benefit from it. Nonetheless, serious and deadly battles still rage; but the Day of the Lord is coming, and the end of our warfare is in sight. The strange numbers listed above may offer an answer to the question posed by the martyred saints, who cry out from beneath the altar, *"How long...Lord?"* (6:10). When does this Day arrive?

Earlier, we noted similarities between Matthew chapter 24 (the Olivet Discourse) and the Book of Revelation. The Discourse, you recall, was in response to the disciples' question, *"what will be the sign of your coming and of the end of the age?"* (Matt. 24:3). Part of Jesus' reply was: *"No one knows about that day or hour, not even the angels in heaven, nor the Son, but only the Father"* (Matt. 24:36).

---
[127] Eller, *War and Peace*, 39.

The Apocalypse does not offer a complete answer to the disciples' question either; we are left to wrestle with symbols, and with asking God for the wisdom to interpret.

We are told that *"the Gentiles ... will trample on the holy city for 42 months"* (11:2), that the two witnesses will *"prophesy for 1,260 days"* (11:3), that God would take care of the woman who had *"fled into the desert ... for a time, times and half a time"* (12:6, 14), and that the sea beast would *"utter proud words and blasphemies"* against God and wage war against the saints for *"forty-two months"* (13:5). Almost all scholars believe that these three terms – "42 months," "1,260 days," and "time, times, and half a time" – are synonyms, and most believe that they may have something to do with the 360-day lunar calendar.

Perhaps the best key to understanding these terms comes from the Book of Daniel. In chapter nine, the prophet was reflecting upon Jeremiah's word: *"the desolation of Jerusalem would last seventy years"* (v. 2; cf. Jer. 25:11). While Daniel was in prayer, the angel Gabriel appeared to him and offered insight:

> *Seventy 'sevens' are decreed for your people and your holy city to finish transgression, to put an end to sin, to atone for wickedness, to bring in everlasting righteousness, to seal up vision and prophecy and to anoint the most holy* (v. 24).

There was to be a decree to *"restore and rebuild Jerusalem,"* and the *"Anointed One"* would come (v. 25), but he would be *"cut off"* after sixty-nine of those "sevens" had run their course (v. 26). During the last of the "sevens," *"He will confirm a covenant with many ... but in the middle of that 'seven' he will put an end to sacrifice and offering"* (v. 27).

Dispensationalist (predictive) scholars[128] believe that the term "seventy 'sevens'" refers to seventy "seven-year periods."[129] Half of a seven-year period would be "42 months," "1,260 days," or "time, times, and half a time." Most scholars, however, believe that

---
[128] See Appendix B.
[129] The Hebrew in v. 24 says, "seventy 'sevens.'" Based on Dan. 9:2 (which does say seventy "years"), Dan. 9:24 is *interpreted* to mean seventy "seven-year periods."

"seventy 'sevens'" is more along the lines of what Jesus said to Peter when the latter asked how many times he should forgive his brother: *"Seventy times seven"* (Matt. 18:22, NKJV), in that case, certainly did not mean 490 times; it meant that one should always forgive. In like manner, the seventy "sevens" in Daniel's text does not mean "490 years;" it most likely refers to some sort of heavenly jubilee (n. Lev. 25:8-13) or state of perfection. There will be an end to transgression and sin; wickedness will be atoned for; and everlasting righteousness will be ushered in, *only* when this state of perfection – i.e. the Day of the Lord – comes.

Based on their method of interpretation, however, Dispensationalist scholars believe that King Artaxerxes (Neh. 2:1-9), in 445 BC, was the one who made the decree *"to restore and rebuild Jerusalem."*[130] The *"Anointed One"* who would be *"cut off"* was a reference to Jesus Christ,[131] and *"the people of the ruler who will come"* (v. 26) refers to the Romans, who destroyed the Temple and the city of Jerusalem in AD 70. Furthermore, there was to be an undetermined length of time between the 69th and 70th week. This gap, known as the "Church Age," would end with the "rapture" (1 Thess. 4:16-18), and then the 70th week of Daniel's prophecy would begin. The 70th week, also known as the seven-year tribulation period (the second half of which is called "the Great Tribulation"), then plays out in Revelation chapters 4-19.

There are several problems with this interpretation. First of all, the decree to which Daniel refers is most likely the one made in 538 BC, by Cyrus, king of Persia (Isaiah 44:28; 45:1, 13; 2 Chr. 36:22-23; Ezra 1).[132] Using 538 BC as a start date for seventy "seven-year periods," the crucifixion would have taken place around 64 BC, a date unacceptable to all. Another huge problem with the predictive approach is the concept of inserting a "Church Age" in between

---

[130] Scofield, 886.

[131] Sixty-nine "seven-year periods" – 483 years – dated from 445 BC, would bring us to AD 38. In making some minor adjustments to the calculations (i.e. 365-day years instead of 360-day years), we could arrive at a fairly plausible date for the crucifixion.

[132] Artaxerxes did not actually issue a decree. He merely gave permission for his cupbearer, Nehemiah, to return to his native Jerusalem. The Book of 1 Esdras (2:1) also makes mention of a decree by Cyrus; Artaxerxes is never mentioned.

the 69th and 70th "seven." There is nothing in the text to justify such an action. Theologians often refer to such methods of interpretation as "eisegesis" – reading into the text things that are not there. Finally, Dispensationalism can lead easily to date setting. Once the rapture happens, there will be exactly seven years until the return of Jesus Christ.

More traditional interpretations suggest that Antiochus IV Epiphanes, king of the Greek Seleucids (175-164 BC), was the *"ruler"* of *"the people ... who will come."* In 175 BC, Onias III, the High Priest of the Temple, *"the Anointed One,"*[133] was *"cut off"* – murdered (2 Macc. 4:36). Antiochus later plundered the Temple in 169 BC, dedicated it to the Greek god Zeus and allowed prostitution on the precincts (2 Macc. 6:2-4). Josephus mentions that he routinely sacrificed swine on the altar.[134] Daniel may have been using the concept of jubilee – seventy 'sevens' – in looking forward to the time when these Greeks would be overthrown, and a perfect Jewish era would set in. The *"one who causes desolation,"* however, would continue, *"until the end that is decreed is poured out on him"* (v. 27).

When John recorded these strange numbers in the Apocalypse, he may have been reflecting upon the similarities between the Greek defilement of the Temple in 169 BC, and Rome's destruction of it in A.D. 70 (n. Matt. 24:15). Early readers of Revelation, no doubt, caught the connection, and like the Jews of Antiochus' day, were looking forward to an era when the yoke of an oppressive empire would be shattered. They longed for that perfect "jubilee," when *"the kingdom of the world"* would *"become the kingdom of our Lord and of his Christ* (11:15). Daniel 9, therefore, may offer some insight into the strange numbers of Revelation, but not as much as the Dispensationalist suggests.

The expression "time, times, and half a time," occurs on two other occasions outside of the Book of Revelation, and both of these are found in the Book of Daniel, as well. The first occurs in chapter

---

[133] The High Priest was always referred to in this manner (see pp. 37-38).
[134] Flavius Josephus, *Jewish Antiquities, Books XII-XIV*, vol. 7, trans. Ralph Marcus (Cambridge, MA: Harvard University Press, 1943), 131.

seven, during Daniel's dream of the four beasts that rose up out of the sea. When *"the Ancient of Days took his seat"* (v. 9), the fourth beast *"was slain and its body destroyed and thrown into the blazing fire."* Before this was to happen, however, the saints would be *"handed over to him for a time, times and half a time."* If the fourth beast of Daniel is the same as the sea beast of Revelation (n. pp. 124-128), the expression "time, times and half a time" refers to the long reign of this beast upon the earth – from the time of Adam, until the day it lands in the lake of fire (Rev. 19:20).

Later in Daniel's prophecy, *"a man dressed in linen, with a belt of the finest gold around his waist"* (Dan. 10:5) appeared to the prophet and helped him to understand a dream that *"concerned a great war"* (10:1). This angelic being was sent to him (10:10) *"to explain … what will happen to your people in the future"* (10:14). Following the description that unfolded in chapters eleven and twelve, Daniel saw two more angelic beings standing on either side of the river. One of them asked the question, *"How long will it be before these astonishing things are fulfilled?"* The man clothed in linen responded, *"It will be for a time, times and half a time"* (Dan. 12:6-7). As in the first example, the expression appears to refer to an indeterminate amount of time.

The expression "42 months" is not used outside of the Book of Revelation, but "42" may have some symbolic significance in other parts of the Bible. In Numbers chapter 33, there are forty-two recorded stages in Israel's journey from Egypt, the land of bondage, to Canaan, the land of promise. In the genealogy of Jesus Christ, presented in the Gospel of Matthew, there are forty-two generations from Abraham, who is the father of the faithful, to Christ, who is the object of our faith (Matt. 1:17).

It is this writer's conclusion, that the expressions "1,260 days," "42 months," and "time, times and half a time" are synonymous and symbolic. Each refers to an indeterminate amount time, which began with Adam's expulsion from Eden, and will end at an hour that "no one knows." During this period, the servants of God are not in complete control of the world,¹³⁵ and spiritual warfare rages. The two witnesses are prophesying; the Gentiles (those who resist our God)¹³⁶ are trampling on the holy city (the world over which the people of God should be ruling), while the woman clothed with the sun (the people of God) is living in the desert, protected by the Most High. At an unknown hour, the Day of the Lord will arrive; the time of our spiritual warfare will cease, and the General will return with *the armies of heaven* (Rev. 19:14) arrayed behind Him. The remaining sections of this chapter will suggest a possible scenario as to how the Day of the Lord might unfold.

the beast that comes up from the Abyss ... (11:7-14)
During times of war, heads of state have been known to release dangerous criminals from prison in hopes that they might use their wrath and cunning against enemy soldiers.¹³⁷ This may be the scenario employed by our King as the Day of the Lord commences. He often uses evil to punish evil (n. Isa. 10:5ff; Jer. 1:14ff.). With the opening of the sixth seal (discussion follows below),¹³⁸ the Abyss is opened, and demons from hell are released upon the earth.

---

¹³⁵Eller, *The Most Revealing Book*, 117, writes: ' "3 ½" is a broken "7," thus itself the number of Evil and thus, for John, the length of the end-time.'
¹³⁶See p. 118
¹³⁷In October 2002, Saddam Hussein, President of Iraq, "ordered ... that all prisoners be released, including non-Iraqi Arabs, with the exception of those accused of spying for the United States or Israel" – this just prior to immanent U.S. invasion; available from http://archives.cnn.com/2002/WORLD/meast/10/20/iraq.amnesty/; Internet.
Arthur L. Frothingham, "Bolshevism," *Handbook of War Facts and Peace Problems* (1919), 4, records how, at the height of the Russian revolution, Boshevist leaders emptied the prisons, freeing 260,000 criminals. These were "either enrolled in the Red Army or made Bolshevist employees and agents." Available from http://www.lib.byu.edu/~rdh/wwi/comment/WarFacts/wfacts6.htm; Internet.
¹³⁸ Again, the similarities with Matthew chapter 24 are fascinating. The contents of the sixth seal (Rev. 6:12-17) seem to parallel Jesus' description of the "great distress" in Matt. 24:21.

The Day Of The Lord (Armageddon)

The Abyss is the haunt of demons. It is the place where enemy POWs are kept, and where Satan is bound with a great chain (20:1-3). Our General placed him there on Good Friday (Col. 2:15), along with many of his henchmen (2 Pet. 2:4; Jude 6). Although multitudes of demons still roam the earth (and they make our lives very difficult), they fear the Abyss and do not want to be sent there (Luke 8:31). On the Day of the Lord, however, the Abyss will be opened up,[139] and God will employ these legions of darkness to punish the inhabitants of the earth – those who reject the love of God. Even Satan will be "*set free for a short time ... to deceive the nations*" (20:3, 8; cf. 2 Thess. 2:3-8).

In this text, some sort of beast rises up out of the Abyss (could this be Apollyon of 9:11; cf. 17:8?), overpowers the two witnesses and kills them. "*Their bodies will lie*[140] *in the street of the great city ... where also their Lord was crucified*" (v. 8),[141] and the inhabitants of the earth will gloat and "*celebrate by sending each other gifts*" (v. 10). This passage is very troubling, especially if we understand the two witnesses to be a symbol of the Church. Will the Church die? Is this what Jesus means when He says: "*when the Son of Man comes, will he find faith on the earth?*" (Luke 18:8). The death of the two witnesses probably refers to the end of the Church's corporate ministry. It does not address the fate of individual believers. (The reader will recall the sealed foreheads of the servants of God in 7:3, protecting them from the coming destruction.) When the Day of

---

[139] The sounding of the fifth (9:1-11) and sixth trumpets (9:13-21), and the pouring out of the sixth bowl (16:12-14) all appear to unleash hideous, demonic creatures from the bowels of the earth.

[140] The Greek "ptoma" often means "fallen in battle."

[141] Many believe that the text refers to the city of Jerusalem. But as Wilcock (106) points out, the city is *figuratively* called Sodom and Egypt. It is better to view this metaphorically than geographically. It was the world, "*the inhabitants of the earth*" (v. 10), the city of man, which put Christ on the cross. Sodom, as a place of horrible depravity (Gen. 19:4-11), and Egypt, as a place of bondage and oppression, are excellent terms to describe the wickedness of this city. The expression "great city" is used several times in the Book of Revelation, but always in the context of "Mystery Babylon," who consistently opposes and puffs herself up against the true and the living God (16:19; 18: 10, 16, 18, 19, 21). It was Babylon who crucified Christ, your sin and mine.

the Lord arrives, the Church, the mighty human army our King has used to bring the gospel message into the world, will no longer be needed. The earth people will rejoice, because no one will be around to remind them of their evil ways. For *"three and a half days"* (v. 9), the witnesses will lie dead in the street,[142] but then suddenly, *"a breath of life from God"* will enter them; they will stand on their feet and go *"up to heaven in a cloud"* (vv. 11-12; 1 Thess. 4:16-18). Satan's apparent victory over the Church, not unlike his "victory" over Christ at Calvary, will be brief. As the two witnesses ascend into heaven, terror will fill the hearts of the earth people. The dragon and his lowly henchmen will turn on them and unleash their wrath with incredible fury. The passage ends with *"a severe earthquake"* that kills seven thousand people and destroys a tenth of the city (v. 13; cf. Zech. 14:3-5).

I watched as he opened the sixth seal ... (6:12-17)
The 1991 Gulf War was one of the most lopsided victories in military history. For the citizens of Iraq, it probably felt as if a terrible earthquake had devastated the country. At 3:00 a.m. on 17 January 1991, 668 coalition aircraft attacked the nation. An F-117 Stealth Fighter began the assault by dropping a 2,000 pound laser-guided bomb onto a telecommunications center "vital to Iraqi military command and control." "EC-130H Compass Call electronic warfare aircraft jammed communications, hindering the effectiveness of Iraq's already crumbling" air defense network. "Microwave towers, telephone relay exchanges, cables, and land line – had been transformed into rubble." The Iraqi Air Force was not a factor; its planes remained in underground bunkers. Saddam Hussein's en-

---

[142]There is probably some sort of symbolic meaning to the term "three and a half *days.*" When compared to the Church's three and one half *years* (42 months, etc) of ministry, three and one half days would be a rather insignificant period of time. John's Gospel suggests that Jesus conducted three years of ministry when He walked the earth. For three days, He lay dead in the "street of the great city," before the "breath of life from God" entered him, snatching Him up to heaven (12:5).

The Day Of The Lord (Armageddon)

tire command and control structure had been destroyed, and "by the time dawn broke ... Iraq was well on the way to losing the war ... A humane leader would have sued for peace."[143]

The next wave of aerial bombardment took out power generation plants, refineries (Iraq was sitting on 20% of the world's known oil reserves at the time), and the transportation infrastructure (41 of the nation's 54 bridges had been destroyed). There was still no surrender. A third wave was launched to "flush out" Iraqi aircraft that remained hidden in shelters. 375 out of 594 shelters, each designed to withstand a nuclear attack, were destroyed, along with the bulk of the Iraqi Air Force. This phase also involved the destruction of enemy tanks, mechanized vehicles, and artillery. Surveillance aircraft were able to locate many of the skillfully camouflaged ground-based weapons systems, and F-111F Aardvark aircraft locked on and destroyed them with laser guided bombs. These planes were achieving up to "150 armor kills *per night*."[144]

---

[143] "Air Power in the Gulf War," *Essays on Air and Space Power,* vol. II, 69-71 passim; available from http://www.globalsecurity.org/military/library/report/1999/air-power-v2-5.pdf; Internet.
[144] Ibid., 71, 74, 75-77, passim.

"Many Iraqi divisions suffered severely under coalition air attack ... over time, the effective strength ... sank to about the 50 percent combat strength level." 109,876 sorties were made during the 43-day war, dropping 84,200 tons of bombs. Stealth Fighters, A-6 Intruders, F-18 Hornets, F-14 Tomcats, AV-8B Harriers, B-52 bombers, F-15E Strike Eagles, F-16 Falcons, and A-10 Warthogs rained down a living hell on the Iraqi military. "The fourth phase of Desert Storm opened at 4:00 a.m. local time, 24 February." By the time the I Marine Expeditionary Force, the XVII Airborne Corps and the VII Armored Corps had maneuvered their men into position to launch the ground war, Iraqi soldiers surrendered, nearly en masse. Mercifully, the ground war was over in one hundred hours. One Iraqi troop commander, interrogated after the war, stated he surrendered 'because of the B-52 strikes. "But your position was *never* attacked by B-52s," the interrogator exclaimed. "That is true," the prisoner replied, "but I saw one that *had* been attacked."'[145]

When the Lamb opens the sixth seal, the real action begins. The Day of the Lord is at hand. Even though the great War Scroll is not yet completely unfurled, its ultimate contents become evident. A great earthquake disorients the inhabitants of the earth. The sun turns black; the moon turns red; stars fall to the earth, and the sky rolls up like a scroll. Similarities with the Olivet Discourse are again noteworthy (Mt. 24:29; cf. Is. 34:2-4). Kings, princes, generals, rich and poor, slave and free *"hid in caves and among the rocks of the mountains."* They cried out to the rocks and to the mountains,

> *Fall on us and hide us from the face of him who sits on the throne and from the wrath of the Lamb! For the great day of their wrath has come, and who can stand (v. 17)?*

In quick succession, wave after wave of destruction will come upon the inhabitants of the earth.[146] The snapping of the seventh seal (8:1) quickly follows the opening of the sixth. When the scroll

---
[145] Ibid, 72, 77-82, passim.
[146] I now use the future tense, because I do not believe these events have occurred. John is given a glimpse of the future. *"On the Lord's Day,"* (Day of the Lord?) He was *"in the Spirit"* (1:10).

is finally unfurled, a series of seven trumpet judgments (8:7-9:21; 11:15) rain down upon the earth. The sounding of the seventh trumpet will be followed up by a wave of seven bowl judgments (16:1-21). In the end, the enemy army will be completely annihilated. There will be no hiding from our General, as every evil will be destroyed forever. There may, however, be lulls in the action, affording the earth people opportunities to repent (16:9).

As we examine some of the images below, we remind ourselves not to be theologically dogmatic. No one knows when the Day of the Lord will arrive, how long it will last, or exactly how it will unfold. We also need to remind ourselves that the Book of Revelation in no way serves as justification for human military action. The examples of modern warfare serve only to illustrate some of the frightening images of the Apocalypse. It does seem very clear, however, that we should align ourselves with our Lord and with His Christ (11:15). It behooves each of us to look inwardly and ask the question, "In whose army am I serving?"

When he opened the seventh seal ... (8:1-5)
Lt. Carey Cash served as chaplain for the men of the First Battalion, Fifth Marine Regiment (1/5) during Operation Iraqi Freedom in 2003. His unit was "the first ground combat force to cross the line of departure into Iraq, saw the first man killed in action at the hands of enemy gunmen, and fought what many believe to have been the most decisive battle in taking Baghdad."[147] A key moment for 1/5 happened at 5:00 p.m. local time in Kuwait on March 20, 2003. A little yellow piece of paper, containing an urgent message from higher headquarters, was handed to the unit's Commanding Officer. The CO 'read the note, took a deep breath ... and said, "It's now. We're crossing the breach now." The response was complete silence.' The battalion commander asked the chaplain for prayer. "After all the training, all the physical conditioning hikes, all the strategy sessions, all the intelligence briefs, all the live-fire rifle ranges, it had come to this – a decisive moment

---
[147] Lt. Carey H. Cash, *A Table in the Presence*, (Nashville, Tennessee: W Publishing Group, 2004), xi-xii.

and a sincere prayer ... In the quiet moments that followed our prayer together," Cash writes, "I was reminded, by a voice too deep for words, that we were not alone."[148]

A dramatic pause precedes the opening of the seventh seal (cf. Josh. 6:10; Hab. 2:20; Zeph. 1:7; Zech. 2:13), a primeval silence before the dawn of a new creation. One might even say that a command comes from on high. The time is now! After all of the messages to the Church, after all of the justifications for war, after all of the school circles and intelligence assessments, the hour has come. The seventh seal is about to be opened. The heavenly creatures are sobered as they viewed the horrible contents of the two-sided scroll. "*There was silence in heaven for about half an hour*" (v. 1). As John gazes in on this heavenly scene, he notices "*the seven angels who stand before God ...were given seven trumpets*" (v. 2).[149] Before they begin sounding them, "*another angel, who had a golden censer ... was given much incense*" (v. 3). This angel then "*took the censer, filled it with fire from the altar, and hurled it on the earth*" (v. 5; cf. Ezek. 10:2). The prayers of those who were under the altar were about to be answered.

seven trumpets/seven bowls (8:6-9:21; 11:15-19; 16:1-14, 17-21)
As wave after wave of air attack pummeled the Iraqi landscape during the 1991 Gulf War, many of the targets were hit two and three times, each strike resulting in ever worsening destruction. There seems to be something similar going on with the trumpet and plague judgments that play out on the Day of the Lord. Trumpet #1 (8:7) resulted in the destruction of 1/3 of the earth; bowl #1 (16:2) also destroyed the earth. Trumpet #2 (8:8-9) resulted in 1/3 of the seas turning into blood and in the death of 1/3 of the creatures living in it; bowl #2 (16:3) was also poured out on the sea, resulting in the death of *every* living sea creature. Trumpet #3 (8:10-11) resulted in 1/3 of the rivers turning bitter; bowl #3 (16:4-7) is also poured out on the rivers, "*and they turned to blood.*" This

---
[148]Ibid., 23-25 passim.
[149]It may be that these seven angels are identical to the "*seven spirits before his throne*" (1:4).

The Day Of The Lord (Armageddon)

pattern continues throughout the cycles of judgment. The trumpet judgments appear to destroy 1/3 of the designated targets, while the bowl judgments bring about their complete destruction. As we move from one judgment to the next, their descriptions lengthen. We need only one verse to describe the devastations of the first trumpet, but eight are needed to describe the havoc wrought by trumpet number six. The seventh trumpet does not even have a clear ending. It may be that its sound reverberates through the bowl judgments and into the description of the new heaven and the new earth of Revelation chapter 21. As noted above, there are pauses between the events of the sixth and seventh judgments, where God speaks to His troops.

There also appears to be great similarities between the trumpet and bowl judgments of the Apocalypse and the plagues of Exodus. As God saw the misery of the Israelites in the land of Egypt, and as he heard their cries (Exod. 3:7), He sent His servant Moses to deliver them from Pharoah and from the land of bondage. As God hears the cries of those from underneath the altar (6:9) and of those going through great tribulation (7:14), He sends His servant Jesus to bring deliverance from Satan and from the bondage of sin and death. As the deliverance of Israel was preceded by plagues upon the unbelieving Egyptians, so the deliverance of all who hunger for the true and the living God will be preceded by plagues upon the inhabitants of the earth. The chart on the next page should prove helpful in analyzing the trumpet and bowl judgments.

The sounding of the seventh trumpet, it seems, is very significant. Its blast was accompanied by loud voices in heaven, which said:

> *The kingdom of the world has become the kingdom of our Lord and of his Christ, and he will reign for ever and ever* (11:15).

Trumpet #	Result	Bowl #	Result	Exodus plague #
1 – hail/blood/fire upon the earth (8:7)	1/3 of earth burned 1/3 of trees burned all grass destroyed	1 – poured out on the land (16:2)	Painful sores on those who worshiped the beast	6, 7 – boils, hail (Exod. 9:8-35)
2 – fiery mountain cast into the sea (8:8-9)	1/3 of sea to blood 1/3 of sea creatures die, 1/3 ships sunk	2 – poured out on the sea (16:3)	Sea turned into blood; every living thing in the sea dies.	1 – river to blood (Exod. 7:20-21)
3 – "Wormwood" star falls from the sky into the waters (8:10-11)	1/3 of fresh water turns bitter	3 – poured out on the rivers (16:4-7)	Rivers turned to blood	1 – river to blood (Exod. 7:20-21)
4 – one third of sun, moon, and stars are darkened (8:12-13)	1/3 of day without light; 1/3 of night without light	4 – poured out on the sun (16:8-9)	The sun scorches people with fire; they refuse to repent	9 – darkness (Exod. 10:21-23)
5 – a star falls to the earth (9:1-12)	The Abyss opened; demon locusts plague the earth	5 – poured out on the throne of the beast (16:10-11)	Mankind tormented; they curse the God of heaven	8 – locusts (Exod. 10:1-20)
6 – release of four angels bound at Euphrates (9:13-21)	200,000,000 mounted troops; 1/3 of mankind killed	6 – poured out on the Euphrates River (16:12-14)	River dries up; Kings of the East/Frog Demons, prepare for battle	10 – death to firstborn (Exod. 11-12)
7 – loud voices in heaven (11:15-?)	God's Temple in Heaven opened. Lightning, thunder, earthquakes	7 – poured out into the air (16:17-?)	A loud voice from the throne. Lightning, thunder, earthquake	Lightning, thunder, trumpet blasts from Mt. Sinai (Exod. 19:16-19)

The Day Of The Lord (Armageddon)

In the Jewish faith, there are three major feast days: the Feast of Unleavened Bread (Passover), the Feast of Harvest (Pentecost), and the Feast of Ingathering (Tabernacles) (see Exod. 23:14-17). Passover occurred when God miraculously delivered the Israelites from the bondage of Egyptian captivity, allowing them to begin a long journey to the Promised Land (Exod. 12). The slaughtering of a lamb and the spreading of its blood upon the doorposts of Jewish homes secured Divine protection. In later years, lambs were sacrificed every spring to commemorate the event. Christians understand Jesus to be the Passover Lamb, *"who takes away the sin of the world!"* (John 1:29; cf. 1 Cor. 5:7-8).

Pentecost (also known as the "Feast of Weeks," or "First Fruits") occurred fifty days after the Passover celebration (Lev. 23:16; cf. Exod. 34:22; Num. 28:26). It was a time when the winter wheat was harvested, when the "first fruits" of the growing season were brought into the barn, and when farmers could relax from their labors. Metaphorically, there is also a harvest of souls. Jeremiah mentions that Israel was "holy to the LORD, the firstfruits of his harvest" (Jer. 2:3). Christians believe that those who follow Jesus, from all nations of the world, are also part of this harvest. Fifty days after the resurrection of Jesus Christ (a day now referred to as Pentecost Sunday), God poured out His Spirit on all people, gathering for Himself the first fruits of a harvest of souls that continues to the present time (Acts 2; cf. Rom. 11:16; 1 Cor. 15:20).

The feast most relevant to our discussion, however, is that of Tabernacles (also known as the "Feast of the Ingathering," or "Booths"). Tabernacles took place in the seventh month of the Jewish calendar, after all of the crops had been harvested. Long, haunting trumpet blasts were sounded upon its commencement. The Israelites were to *"take choice fruit from the trees, and palm fronds, leafy branches and poplars, and rejoice before the LORD"* (Lev. 23:23-44). It was a time to thank God for His bounty. Just as Christians see the feasts of Passover and Pentecost fulfilled by Jesus Christ, many believe that a day is coming when the fulfillment of the Feast of Tabernacles will be announced by a *"trumpet call ... and the dead in Christ will rise"* (1 Thess. 4:16; cf. 1 Cor. 15:52;

Zech. 14:16ff.). The seventh trumpet of the Apocalypse could be the very same trumpet blast to which the Apostle Paul was referring in 1 Thess. 4 and 1 Cor. 15. When it sounds, the harvesters will *"collect the weeds and tie them in bundles to be burned"* and then gather the wheat and bring it into the Lord's barn (Matt. 13:30; Rev. 14:15). There is an old hymn entitled: "When the Roll is Called up Yonder." Its first verse follows:

> When the trumpet of the Lord shall sound
> and time shall be no more
> And the morning breaks eternal, bright and fair —
> When the saved of earth shall gather over on the other shore
> And the roll is called up yonder I'll be there.[150]

It would be a good thing for each of us to ask the question: "Where will I be on the Day when the Lord's trumpet sounds?"

The Three Angels (14:6-11)
Many things follow the blast of the seventh trumpet: descriptions of friendly and enemy combatants (chaps. 12-14; 17; 19), seven bowls of God's wrath (chaps. 15-16), and the destruction of enemy forces (chaps. 18-20). In the midst of the blast there are three angels, Divine Heralds, *"flying in midair."* The first one proclaims the *"eternal gospel ... to those who live on the earth – to every nation, tribe, language and people"* (v. 6). He urges us to *"Worship him who made the heavens, the earth, the sea and the springs of water"* (v. 7). Wilcock suggests that the "eternal gospel" is that which was "preached to Adam in Eden, before the relationship had ever been spoilt; it is the hypothetical gospel with which Christ challenged the lawyer in Luke 10:28 – 'Do this, and you will live' ... 'Recognize God as Creator and Judge, the Beginning and End of your existence, and all will be well.'"[151] Even in the throes of final judgment, our great King is appealing to his creation to repent and follow Him.

---

[150]"When the Roll Is Called Up Yonder," Text and Music: James M. Black, *THE HYMNAL for Worship & Celebration.* (Waco, Texas: WORD MUSIC, 1986), #543.
[151]Wilcock, 134.

The Day Of The Lord (Armageddon)

The second angel announces that Babylon the Great, the harlot who perverted religious worship, has fallen (v. 8). We will read of her destruction below. The third angel again reminds us not to take the mark of the dreadful beast that has risen out of the sea (v. 9). Those who do will *"will drink of the wine of God's fury ... poured full strength into the cup of his wrath"* (v. 10; cf. Job 21:20; Ps. 75:8; Isa 51:17; Jer. 25:15-38). Our General already drank from this cup (Luke 22:42); those who follow Him will not have to drink from it, and will not face the wrath described in this text.

The Harvest of the Earth (14:14-20)

The expression, *"son of man"* (v. 14) was used in chapter one (1:13), when John first met our Commanding General. In this text, the son of man swings into action, making use of a sharp sickle and angelic helpers to harvest the earth (cf. Jer. 51:33; Hos. 6:11). The feast of Tabernacles has come in its fullness. The *"clusters of grapes from the earth's vine"* are thrown into *"the great winepress of God's wrath"*[152] and the *"blood flowed out of the press, rising as high as the horses' bridles for a distance of 1,600 stadia"* (vv. 18-20). Mounce writes that this distance, "1600 furlongs (some 184 miles), has been variously interpreted. Geographically it is the approximate length of Palestine. Symbolically ... (it suggests) the judgment of God ... taking place outside the holy city ... (extending) to all ... who find themselves beyond the pale of divine protection."[153]

---

[152]This passage served as inspiration for the words "He is trampling out the vintage where the grapes of wrath are stored," in Julia W. Howe's "The Battle Hymn of the Republic." Available from http://www.cyberhymnal.org/htm/b/h/bhymnotr.htm; Internet.

[153]Mounce, 283, suggests that by squaring the number four – i.e. the "four corners of the earth," (7:1; 20:8), and the "four winds of the earth," (7:1) – and by multiplying it by the square of ten, "the number of completeness; (5:11; 20:6)," we will arrive at the figure "1600." Another scenario proposes squaring the number "forty" – "the traditional number for punishment (Num 14:33; Deut 25:3)."

the place ... called Armageddon (16:16)
When the sixth angel *"poured out his bowl on the great river Euphrates,"* its waters dried up in order *"to prepare the way for the kings of the East"* (16:12). As mentioned above, these "kings" may have been demons (16:13-14), released from the Abyss at the commencement of the Day of the Lord, with the mission of inflicting punishment upon the inhabitants of the earth. Popular culture often refers to the "Battle of Armageddon," but this is the only time the word "Armageddon" occurs in the Book of Revelation. Mentioned in the midst of the seven plagues that are raining down upon the earth, Armageddon appears to be synonymous with what we have been calling "the Day of the Lord."

"Megiddo" is a Hebrew term that means "place of troops" or "place of slaughter." The *valley* of Megiddo in modern day Israel is approximately 14 miles wide and 20 miles long. Napoleon called it "the most natural battlefield of the whole earth." Throughout history, many campaigns were waged in this valley: Barak destroyed the Canaanites at Megiddo (Judg. 5:19), Gideon and three hundred men defeated the Midianites (Judg. 7), and King Josiah lost his life there (2 Kings 23:29). The valley of Megiddo was used by Titus and the Roman armies to sack Jerusalem, by the crusaders in the Middle Ages, and by the British General Allenby in 1917.[154]

The verse, at which we are looking, however, speaks of *"Har Megiddo,"* which means the *mountain* of Megiddo. As Mounce points out, there is no such place.[155] What is being described, in highly symbolic language, is the "mountain" of all battles, or as we might say, "the mother of all battles." John is not describing a place, but an *event*. A day is coming when the Lord of hosts and His mighty Army will crush the dragon, the beast, the false prophet, and all demonic and human forces that align themselves with this hideous trinity. In the next section, we will take note of the magnitude of this destruction.

---

[154] Wiersbe, 117-118.
[155] Mounce, 301.

The Day Of The Lord (Armageddon)

Fallen! Fallen is Babylon the Great! (18:1-24)
The pernicious influence of Mystery Babylon upon human history was noted above. Here, her destruction is recorded. An angel came down from heaven, and with "*a mighty voice he shouted: Fallen! Fallen is Babylon the Great*" (v. 2)! The people of God are warned to "*come out of her ... for her sins are piled up to heaven*" (vv. 4-5). "*The kings of the earth who committed adultery with her and shared her luxury ... will weep and mourn over her ... they will stand far off and cry:*"

> *Woe! Woe, O great city,*
> *O Babylon, city of power!*
> *In one hour your doom has come!* (vv. 9-10)

Vast descriptions of her enormous wealth fill the page, until finally: '*a mighty angel picked up a boulder the size of a large millstone and threw it into the sea, and said: "With such violence the great city of Babylon will be thrown down, never to be found again"*' (v. 21).

The ancient city of Babylon reached its zenith under the reign of King Nebuchadnezzar, 604-562 BC (n. Dan. 4:30). The Roman historian Herodotus tells us that the city was laid out in an exact square, fifteen miles on a side. A brick wall 87 feet thick and 100 feet high enclosed it (the Babylonians were able to drive six chariots abreast on top of these walls), and the 250 towers on top of the wall served as lookout posts. There was a moat filled with water that surrounded the city, and a second wall running inside the first one. Inside were twenty-five magnificent avenues, each 150' wide, running from north to south, and twenty-five more running from east to west. The Euphrates River flowed through the city, cutting it in half. A bridge spanned the river, with an ornate palace at each end, "connected by a subterranean passageway ... underneath the bed of the river, in which at different points were located sumptuous banqueting rooms constructed entirely of brass."[156]

---

[156] Larkin, 155 passim.

Near one of the palaces was the tower of Bel, one of the seven wonders of the ancient world, which stood 660 feet high. An exterior staircase wound its way to the top of the structure, where there was a chapel that contained the "most expensive furniture of any place of worship in the world." One of the golden images in the chapel stood 45 feet high; the sacred utensils used in worship were priceless. Another one of the seven wonders of the ancient world, the hanging gardens of Babylon, built by Nebuchadnezzar to please his wife, were also located within the city. These were four hundred feet square at the base, and rose in terraces to a height of 350'. Staircases, ten feet wide, made their way to the top of the gardens. From a distance, the hanging gardens had the appearance of a forest-covered mountain, which was a "remarkable sight in the level plains of the Euphrates River." The ancient city of Babylon was "probably the most magnificent city the world has ever seen," but as Larkin says, "its fall reveals what a city may become when it forsakes God and He sends His judgment upon it."[157]

In 587 BC, King Nebuchadnezzar, king of Babylon, destroyed the city of Jerusalem and the magnificent temple of the Jewish people. Years before Nebuchadnezzar's reign and his subsequent invasion of Israel, Isaiah the prophet predicted the destruction of his empire: 'And the lookout shouted ... "Look, here comes a man in a chariot with a team of horses. And he gives back the answer: 'Babylon has fallen, has fallen! All the images of its gods lie shattered on the ground!'"' (Isa. 21:8-9; cf. Isa. 13). Jeremiah, a contemporary of Nebuchadnezzar, also predicted Babylon's downfall, recording on a scroll all of the disasters that would come upon her. This he gave to Seraiah, the staff officer of King Zedekiah: *"When you finish reading this scroll, tie a stone to it and throw it into the Euphrates. Then say, 'So will Babylon sink to rise no more because of the disaster I will bring upon her. And her people will fall'"* (51:63-64).

Daniel the prophet records her downfall. As King Belshazzar was eating and drinking with his courtesans (using the golden vessels from the destroyed Jewish temple), he "*praised the gods of gold*

---

[157] Ibid., 156 passim.

and silver, of bronze, iron, wood and stone. Suddenly the fingers of a human hand appeared and wrote on the plaster of the wall." The inscription declared: *"God has numbered the days of your reign and brought it to an end."* Daniel writes: *"that very night Belshazzar, king of the Babylonians, was slain, and Darius the Mede took over the kingdom, at the age of sixty-two"* (Dan. 5:4-5, 26, 30-31). Secular historians tell us the Persian general, Cyrus the Great, diverted the waters of the Euphrates River upstream from the city of Babylon, allowing his troops to enter into the ancient city via the riverbed.[158] The Babylonian kingdom was no more.

John, the scribe of the Apocalypse, clearly referred to these prophesies as he records the destruction of *Mystery* Babylon. The first readers of Revelation, as they pondered what the Emperor Nero and his immediate successor, Vespasian, had done to the second Jerusalem temple in AD 70, surely comforted themselves with thoughts of a coming destruction of the Roman Empire (cf. 1 Pet. 5:13). But as noted above, Babylon appears to be a symbol of religious oppression in any era. As God protected His covenant people during the fall of ancient Babylon, so He will protect His people when Mystery Babylon is destroyed. When Cyrus diverted the waters of the Euphrates, and the Persian army entered the city, God protected His people who lived in its midst. Israel emerged from the destruction, later returned to Jerusalem, and rebuilt the Temple. On a cosmic level, the waters of the Euphrates will once again be cut off (n. Rev. 16:12), and the kings of the earth (demonic armies) will enter the worldly city and destroy it. God will again protect His people. Those who follow Him will emerge from Mystery Babylon unscathed, and enter the New Jerusalem where *"the Lord God Almighty and the Lamb are its temple"* (21:22). As human beings, we should not place our ultimate loyalties in worldly riches or philosophies, because, on the Day of the Lord, these will be thrown like boulders to the bottom of the sea, *"never to be found again"* (v. 21).

---

[158] Ibid., 157.

the fiery lake of burning sulfur ... (19:17-21; 20:7-10)
On the Day of the Lord, *"the beast and the kings of the earth and their armies"* (19:19) will make war against our General and His armies. Satan, recently released from the Abyss (20:7), will lead this final insurrection. Enemy troops will surround *"the camp of God's people,"* but fire will come down from heaven and devour them (20:9). The beast and the false prophet will be captured and *"thrown alive into the fiery lake of burning sulfur"* (19:20). Ultimately, Satan will be thrown into this dreadful place, and the three of them *"will be tormented day and night for ever and ever"* (20:9-10). Those who choose to serve in the enemy army will be *"killed with the sword"* and the birds will gorge themselves on their flesh (19:21).

Jesus declared that the eternal fire was *"prepared for the devil and his angels"* (Matt. 25:41). Much of His earthly ministry was spent warning us not to follow those who would lead us into perdition and the horrors of hell (Matt. 8:12; 22:13; 25:46; Mark 9:48). It is not God's will that any one should perish. The desire of our King's heart is that we should follow Him (1 Tim. 2:4; 2 Pet. 3:9); His mercy is great. As we think of the teachings of the New Testament, and as we reflect upon the judgments that play out in the Book of Revelation, there should be no doubt as to which army we should give our loyalty. Someone once asked Jesus, *"What must we do to do the works God requires?"* Our General responded: *"The work of God is this: to believe in the one he has sent"* (John 6:28-29). In order for us to do the work of God, we must trust Jesus Christ; we must trust Him in the same way that a Private would trust the leadership of his or her commanding general. The appeal found in the last chapter of the Apocalypse is one that invites us to come and follow:

> *The Spirit and the bride say, "Come!" And let him who hears say, "Come!" Whoever is thirsty, let him come; and whoever wishes, let him take the free gift of the water of life (22:17).*

In the next chapter, we shall look at the final judgment (The War Tribunal), and the everlasting peace that will break out after the enemy armies are destroyed.

Chapter 8

THE WAR TRIBUNAL & A LASTING PEACE
(Revelation 20:11-22:6)

"You have conquered, Galilean."[159]
- Julian the Apostate

Then I saw a great white throne ... (20:11-15)
Following World War II, a series of trials were held in Nuremberg, Germany, in which twenty-four Nazi leaders were indicted and tried as war criminals by an international military tribunal. Charges lodged against them included: 1) crimes against peace, 2) crimes against humanity, and 3) violations of the laws of war. Of the twenty-four, two committed suicide while in prison, one was deemed mentally and physically incapable of standing trial, and three were acquitted. Seven received prison sentences (three of which were for life), and eleven were sentenced to death by hanging. In rendering these decisions, the tribunal rejected two major arguments put forth by the defense: 1) "only a state, and not individuals, could be found guilty of war crimes," and 2) the trial and its adjudication were *ex post facto*. The latter defense was rejected on the grounds that "such acts had been regarded as criminal prior to World War II."[160]

---
[159]Peter Jones, *The Gnostic Empire Strikes Back*, (Phillipsburg, New Jersey: P&R Publishing, 1992), 12-13.
[160]Nurnberg trials," *The New Encyclopaedia Britannica* vol. 8, 15th ed., (Chicago: Encyclopaedia Britannica, Inc. 1997), 834 passim.

Following the Day of the Lord, our King conducts a war tribunal. A *"great white throne"* was in place, and John saw *"him who was seated upon it."* (Remember the Captain's Chair, located on the bridge of a ship? In addition to being the seat of authority from which all activities of the warship are controlled, it is also the location from which the Navy's method of executing justice, "Captain's Mast," is often meted out.) *"Earth and sky fled"* from the presence of the One seated upon the throne, and the dead, *"great and small,"* were found standing before Him. *"Books were opened ... (and) the dead were judged according to what they had done"* (v. 12; cf. Dan. 7:10). *"Then death and Hades were thrown into the lake of fire (and) ... if anyone's name was not found written in the book of life, he was thrown into the lake of fire"* (vv. 14-15).

Not all who were guilty of war crimes stood trial at Nuremberg; many escaped the tribunal. Justice in this world is never perfect, but in the next it will be, and none of us will escape the judgment of God (n. Matt. 25:31-46; Acts 17:31; Rom. 14:10; 2 Cor. 5:10; 2 Tim. 4:1). Everything we have ever done is recorded; every evil thought, every sin of omission and of commission is written down. The war waged by our General was against the dragon, the sea beast, and the earth beast. These, along with death and hades, have already landed in the lake of fire (19:20; 20:10). But there is more than just institutional evil. We also have committed crimes against peace, against humanity, and against the laws of war. Our actions, directly or indirectly, both indiscriminately and out of proportion, have contributed to imperialism, war, and famine. Our behavior, in various ways supportive of the sea beast, has contributed to the persecution and death of others. The Law, the prophets, and the apostles have warned us of the consequences of our actions, leaving us without excuse. We are all guilty. On judgment day, when the books are opened, our sins will play out before our eyes.

Fortunately, there is a way out, and that is the thrust of this commentary. There is another book, called the book of life, in which the names of those who serve in the Lamb's Army are recorded.[161] Even though our hands are covered with blood, and we will be

---

[161] See comments on p. 74.

filled with shame as the words of our own book are read, a great General will stand on our behalf – one might say in the role of a defense attorney (n. 1 John 2:1) – and proclaim, 'this one's name is *"written in the book of life"'* (v. 15). Even though my life was not perfect, and I made a lot of errors as a foot soldier in the Army of the Most High, I was following the right General, and He has granted victory.

Then I saw a new heaven and a new earth ... (21:1-27)
After the war is over and the tribunal completed, the people of God will enter a new heaven and a new earth (cf. Isa. 65:17-19), a new Jerusalem (n. Isa. 54:11-12; Gal. 4:25-26; Heb. 11:10; 12:18-23; 13:14). A time of peace will be at hand, never again to be shattered. The work of Christ is complete, the "already" as well as the "not yet" (v. 6; John 19:30). Those who have served in the Army of God are going home; their deployments are over. In this new city, God will wipe the tears from our eyes; there will be *"no more death or mourning or crying or pain"* (v. 4). There will be no more sea (v. 1); that metaphorical place of danger, storm and fear – home to the great beast who blasphemed God and made war against His saints – is gone. He who is seated upon the throne will make everything new (cf. 2 Co. 5:17). As indicated by the chart below, the evil, first recorded in Genesis, is now destroyed forever.

Revelation 20-22	Genesis 1-3
Triumph of the Lamb (20:10; 22:3)	Triumph of the serpent (3:13)
Satan disappears forever (20:10)	Satan appears (3:1)
A new heaven and a new earth (21:1)	Creation of heaven and earth (1:1)
Walk with God restored (21:3)	Walk with God interrupted (3:8-10)
No more pain (21:4)	Pain and sorrow multiplied (3:16)
No more death or sorrow (21:4)	The reality of death (2:17)
Paradise is opened (21:5)	Paradise is closed (3:23)
No need of sun or moon (21:23)	Creation of the sun and moon (1:16)
No more night (21:25)	The darkness is called night (1:5)
Nothing defiles the city (21:27)	Defilement in the garden (3:6-7)
No more curse (22:3)	The ground is cursed (3:17)
They shall see His face (22:4)	Driven from God's presence (3:24)
Man's dominion is restored (22:5)	Man's dominion is lost (3:19)
Access to tree of life reinstated (22:14)	Access to the tree of life denied (3:24)

One of the seven angels took John *"away in the Spirit to a mountain great and high"* (v. 10) and showed him *"the bride, the wife of the Lamb ... the Holy City, Jerusalem, coming down out of heaven from God"* (vv. 9-10).[162] The contrast with the great harlot of chapter seventeen could not be greater! Whereas the great harlot will be thrown as a boulder into the midst of the sea (18:21), the Bride of Christ will dwell in the presence of God forever (21:3). As John describes the beauty of this city, we take note of her twelve gates, upon which *"were written the names of the twelve tribes of Israel"* (v. 12; cf. Ezek. 48:30-34), as well as her twelve foundations upon which were inscribed *"the names of the twelve apostles of the Lamb"* (v. 14; cf. Eph. 2:20).

Earlier in the text, John heard the number of those who were to be protected from the coming judgment: *"144,000 from all the tribes of Israel"* (7:4). In chapter eleven, he was given a reed and told to *"measure the temple of God ... and count the worshipers there"* (11:1). In this chapter, the angel measures *"the city, its gates and its walls"* (v. 15; cf. Ezek. 40:2-3; Zech. 2:1-2), and found it to be *"12,000 stadia in length, and as wide and high as it is long,"* with walls *"144 cubits thick"* (vv. 16-17). Surely, these numbers are not to be taken literally [from a purely engineering standpoint, a wall 216' thick (144 cubits) would not support a height of 1500 miles (12,000 stadia)]; they are symbols, expressing the totality of God's people. 12 (apostles) x 12 (tribes) = 144 (the thickness of the wall).[163] "The Holy City," "the new Jerusalem," and "the Bride of Christ" are terms that describe all who follow our General, both Jew and Gentile. As noted before, the numbers are incalculable; the Holy City is immense in its dimensions.

In this city there is no temple, *"because the Lord God Almighty and the Lamb are its temple"* (v. 22), and there is no need *"for the sun or the moon to shine on it, for the glory of God gives it light, and the Lamb is its lamp"* (v. 23; cf. Zech. 14:6-7). In the Garden of

---

[162]The metaphor of marriage is often used to describe the relationship between Almighty God and His people. Note especially Isa. 54:1-6; 62:5; Jer. 2:2; 3:14; Ezek. 16; Hos. 2:16, 19-23; Matt. 9:15; John 3:28-29; 2 Cor. 11:2; Eph. 5:22-32; Rev. 19:7-9).
[163]See comments on pages 101-104.

Eden there was no temple because God was present, and Adam and Eve enjoyed His company. As a result of their disobedience, however, they (and all of us by proxy) were cast out. But God brought restoration. At first, He appeared to the Israelites from the midst of a moveable tabernacle. Later, when Israel settled in the land of Canaan, our King appeared from the Holy of Holies in the ancient Temple, but only to the High Priest, and only on the Day of Atonement. When Christ came, the dynamic changed. He declared, *"one greater than the temple is here"* (Matt. 12:6). When He died on the cross, *"the curtain of the temple was torn in two from top to bottom"* (Matt. 27:51), symbolically suggesting that the presence of God was no longer limited to the Temple precincts. In fact, the New Testament teaches that those who follow our General *"are the temples of the living God"* (2 Cor. 6:16). His Spirit has taken up residence in our hearts, and He is with us always, even until the end of the age. At the restoration of all things, our transformation will be complete; we will be in the presence of God forever, and there will be no more need of a temple. In like manner, Jesus Christ is the *"light of the world"* (John 8:12; cf. John 1:9), and the *"radiance of God's glory"* (Heb. 1:3). His presence will illumine the heavenly city, and we who follow Him will bask in His glory forever (cf. Isa. 60:11, 19).

Then the angel showed me the river of the water of life ... (22:1-6)
In the first chapter of the Bible, God created the world. In this last chapter, it is recreated. Ezekiel, in looking forward to Israel's return from Babylonian exile, wrote: The *"land that was laid waste has become like the garden of Eden"* (Ezek. 36:35). His words have even deeper meaning as we reflect upon this last chapter of the Apocalypse.

Adam and Eve were cast out of the original garden as a result of their rebellion, but God, in His great mercy, restored paradise. As a river watered the first garden (Gen. 2:10-14), so *"the river of the water of life"* flows *"from the throne of God"* in the new Eden (v. 1; cf. Pss. 1:3; 46:4-5; Jer. 17:7-8; Joel 3:18; Zech. 14:8). During His earthly ministry, Jesus offered living water to all who would drink

(John 4:14; 7:37-38; cf. Ps. 42:1.2). When our combat is over, when we enter this era of eternal peace, the water will be plentiful, refreshing beyond comprehension. As the old hymn declares:

> Like a river glorious Is God's perfect peace, Over all victorious In its bright increase; perfect yet it floweth Fuller eve - 'ry day, Perfect, yet it groweth Deeper all the way.[164]

Does this river flow through your life? Jesus Christ, the Lord of heaven and earth, offers living water. Come and drink from this river that flows from the throne of God.

On either side of this river is the tree of life, *"bearing twelve crops of fruit, yielding its fruit every month."* Its leaves are for the *"healing of the nations"* (v. 2). In the original garden, there were two trees: *"the tree of life and the tree of the knowledge of good and evil"* (Gen. 2:9). Adam was to "stand watch" over Eden, and protect it from the enemy. He was *"free to eat from any tree"* in it, except from *"the tree of the knowledge of good and evil"* (Gen. 2:16-17). Adam failed in his mission, and God removed him from paradise declaring, *"The man has now become like one of us, knowing good and evil. He must not be allowed to reach out his hand and take also from the tree of life and eat, and live forever"* (Gen. 3:22). Cherubim with flaming swords were placed at the entrance of the garden to keep humankind away from the tree of life. (Surely none of us would want to live forever as soldiers in the midst of combat!) Our General, however, was sent as a second Adam (see 1 Co. 15:45), and He was successful in His mission. He destroyed the tempting serpent, and as a result, humans are able to regain access to the tree of life and to its nourishing, healing fruit (n. Ezek. 47:12).

As a result of humanity's rebellion against God, the entire earth was brought under a curse. The serpent was condemned to crawl on its belly and eat dust. Adam was forced to eke out an existence, toiling by the sweat of his brow, cultivating food from soil that pro-

---

[164]"Like a River Glorious" Text: Frances Ridley Havergal; Music: James Mountain; Descant and choral ending by James C. Gibson. *THE HYMNAL for Worship & Celebration.* WORD MUSIC, Waco, Texas, 1986, #494.

duced thorns and thistles. For Eve, the joy of childbirth was now accompanied with great labor pangs, and her husband would rule over her. Ultimately, everything would die. *"For dust you are and to dust you will return"* (Gen. 3:19). Everything outside of the garden was cursed, and even the very last words of the Hebrew Scriptures leave us in despair: *"I will come and strike the land with a curse"* (Mal. 4:6). Much of the business with which we envelop ourselves in this present world is stained with the curse that resulted from Adam's rebellion, but in the new Eden, the curse has been removed. *"No longer will there be any curse. The throne of God and of the Lamb will be in the city, and his servants will serve him* (v. 3). Christ, our General, has *"redeemed us from the curse of the law by becoming a curse for us"* (Gal. 3:13). Not even Moses, the greatest man of the Old Testament, was allowed to see the face of God (Exod. 33:20); but in the new Eden, all who love Him will see Him face to face (v. 4; cf. Matt. 5:8), and will reign with Him forever (v. 5; cf. Dan. 7:18).

EPILOGUE
AND OLD TALES BE RETOLD ...

I, John, am the one who heard and saw these things ... (22:7-21)
I subscribe to a magazine called "*Shipmate*," a monthly journal published by the United States Naval Academy Alumni Association in Annapolis, MD. The section entitled "Class News" takes up approximately two thirds of each issue. Under the subtitle, "*But still when two or three shall meet, And old tales be retold ...,*" members of the various graduating classes tell stories of where their Naval journeys have led them. The January-February 2005 issue goes all the way back to the class of 1924. If one were to read all of the stories these men and women tell, much could be learned about the history of the last century. All of the graduates were, at some point, recruited into the Naval service; each went through boot camp (at the Naval Academy, the experience is called "Plebe year)," and most were commissioned, serving at least a couple of years on board ships or with battalions of Marines. Many of the graduates fought in wars for their country, and some were even involved in tribunals. All of the graduates have longed for peace. Hopefully, most of them have found the inner peace described in this book, but none of them has yet seen the eschatological peace that only God can bring.

As John concludes his masterpiece, he speaks as a veteran warrior. He has seen and participated in things that no one else has experienced. In his conclusion, he leaves us with his most important thoughts. First of all, Jesus Christ is coming soon (vv. 7, 12, 20); *"the time is near"* (v. 10); no one knows when, but all of us must be ready. Secondly, we are to *"Worship God"* (v. 9; cf. 19:10). The earth beast and the sea beast continually vie for our deepest allegiance, and many other things can become idolatrous as well. (In John's case, even the angel who was showing him these things!) Only the great General who has overcome these enemies is worthy of our worship. Thirdly, John offers ministry advice: we are not to *"seal up the words of ... this book"* (v. 10) or change them in any way (v. 18). God's battle plan is for all to see; it is no longer a "Top Secret" document. All who are acquainted with its contents are left without excuse. As warriors for the Most High, we boldly share His word, but do not coerce. *"Let him who does wrong continue to do wrong ... let him who does right continue to do right ..."* (v. 11). Those who serve our General come to Him freely; His is an all-volunteer force. Finally, John extends an invitation. '*The Spirit and the bride* (the Church) *say, "Come!" Whoever is thirsty, let him come; and whoever wishes, let him take the free gift of the water of life*' (v. 18; cf. Isa. 55:1-3). You, the reader, are invited to serve in this mighty Army, for the Captain, indeed, is on the bridge. *"The grace of the Lord Jesus be with God's people. Amen"* (v. 21).

APPENDICES

Appendix A –
Angels in the Book of Revelation

Type	Examples in Revelation	Other Biblical Examples
Messenger angels	1:1; 22:8 (angel speaks to John)	Dan. 8:16-26; 9:20-27; Luke 1:19, 26-38 (Gabriel)
Guardian angels	1:20; 7:1 (angels of the 7 churches; angels hold back the 4 winds)	Num. 22:21-41; Dan. 10:5-21; Matt.18:10; Acts 12:7, 15 (Balaam, Daniel and Peter's angels)
Worship angels	4:6; 5:11 (around the throne)	Exod. 25:18-20; Heb.8:5; Isa. 6:2-3; Ezek.1:5-9; Dan. 7:10
Divine Heralds	5:2; 8:2; 10:1-3; 14:6-10; 18:21-24; 19:17 (seven angels w/ trumpets)	Matt. 24:31; 1 Thess. 4:16 (the voice of an archangel, the trumpet call of God)
Fallen angels	9:16; 12:4; 12:9; 20:7-9 (flung to the earth, locked in the Abyss)	Isa. 14:12-15; Ezek. 28:12-19; Dan. 8:5-10; Matt. 12:29; 25:41; Luke 8:31; 10:18-20; John 12:31-32; Col. 2:15; 2 Thess. 2:3-8; Jude 6 (the strong man; the man of sin; Lucifer; Satan; the prince of this world)
Warrior angels	12:7; 20:1-2 (Michael)	2 Kings 19:32-35; Matt. 26:53; Jude 9 (185,000 Assyrians destroyed; twelve legions of angels)
Angels of Judgment	14:17; 15:1(angel with sickle; angels with bowls of God's wrath)	Gen. 19:1,13; Matt. 13:41-42 (Sodom and Gomorrah; the fiery furnace)

Appendix B –
Millennial Views
(A Chronological Presentation)

HISTORIC PREMILLENNIALISM: (1) The millennium is in the future. (2) The world gets progressively worse. The Church "saves souls," has very little impact upon the institutions of the world, and undergoes much tribulation (Rev. 4-19 describes the downward spiral of wickedness). (3) The Second Coming of Christ, and the battle of Armageddon (19:11-21) (4) The resurrection of the righteous (20:4) (4a) Christ's *literal* and *political* thousand-year reign on earth (20:1-6) (4b) The unleashing and judgment of Satan (20:7-10) (4c) The resurrection of the unrighteous (20:12) (5) The judgment of the righteous and of the unrighteous (20:11-15) (6) New heaven/new earth (Rev. 21-22)

DISPENSATIONAL PREMILLENNIALISM: (1) The millennium is in the future. (2) The world gets progressively worse. The Church "saves souls," has little impact upon the institutions of the world, and undergoes some tribulation (Rev. 4-19 describes a future period of "Great Tribulation" that impacts *only* non-believers). (2a) The Church is suddenly "raptured" out of the world (4:1), with God now working through the restored nation of Israel. (2b) Seven years of tribulation afflict the earth (as unfolded in Rev. 4-19). (3) The Second Coming of Christ, and the battle of Armageddon (19:11-21) (3a) Christ's *literal* and *political* thousand year reign on earth (20:1-6) (3b) The unleashing and judgment of Satan (20:7-10) (4) the last in a series of resurrections (20:12) (5) The last in a series of judgments (20:11-15) (6) New heaven/new earth (Rev. 21-22)

POSTMILLENNIALISM: (1) We are already living in the millennium, symbolically understood. (2) The world improves. The Church "saves souls," has a great impact upon the institutions of the world, and undergoes much tribulation (the events of Rev. 4-19 have already taken place). (3) The Second Coming of Christ, the unleashing of Satan, the battle of Armageddon, and the destruction of Satan and his cohorts occur quickly at the end of the age (described *only* in 20:7-10). (4) Resurrection of the righteous and the unrighteous (20:12) (5) Judgment of the righteous and of the unrighteous (20:11-15) (6) New heaven/new earth (Rev. 21-22)

AMILLENNIALISM: (1) We are already living in the millennium, symbolically understood. (2) The world stays pretty much the same; good and evil coexist alongside of each other. The Church "saves souls," has some impact upon the institutions of the world, and undergoes much tribulation (the events of Rev. 4-19 are ongoing realities). (3) The Second Coming of Christ, the unleashing of Satan, the battle of Armageddon, and the destruction of Satan and his cohorts occur quickly at the end of the age (described variously in 6:12-17; 16:12-21; 19:11-21; 20:7-10). (4) Resurrection of the righteous and the unrighteous (20:12) (5) Judgment of the righteous and of the unrighteous (20:11-15) (6) New heaven/new earth (Rev. 21-22)

BIBLIOGRAPHY

Adams, Jay. *The Time is at Hand*. Nutley, NJ: Presbyterian and Reformed Publishing Co., 1977.

"Air Power in the Gulf War." *Essays on Air and Space Power*, vol. 2: 69-71. Database on-line. Available from http://www.globalsecurity.org/militarylibrary/report/1999/airpower-v2-5.pdf; Internet.

Allen, Joseph L. *War, A Primer for Christians*. Dallas: The Cary M. Maguire Center for Ethics and Public Responsibility and Southern Methodist University Press, 1991.

Aune, David E. *Revelation 17-22*. Word Biblical Commentary, vol. 52c. Nashville: Thomas Nelson Publishers, 1998.

Book of Worship For United States Forces: A collection of Hymns and Worship *Resources for Military Personnel of the United States of America*. Washington, DC: U.S. Government Printing Office, 1974.

Boswell, James. *Life of Johnson*. 1970. Database on-line. Available from http://www.bartleby.com/73/1306.html; Internet.

Brown, Raymond E., Joseph A. Fitzmyer, and Roland E. Murphy, eds. *The New Jerome Bible Handbook*. Collegeville, MN: The Liturgical Press, 1992.

Cahill, Lisa Sowle. *Love Your Enemies: Discipleship, Pacifism, and Just War Theory*. Minneapolis: Fortress Press, 1994.

Cash, Carey H. *A Table in the Presence*. Nashville, TN: W. Publishing Group, 2004.

Department of State. "America Must Remain Engaged." *Dispatch* 51 (21 December 1992).

Eller, Vernard. *The Most Revealing Book of the Bible: Making Sense out of Revelation*. Grand Rapids: William B. Eerdmans Publishing Company, 1974.

_____. *War and Peace from Genesis to Revelation*. Scottdale, PA and Kitchener, Ontario: Herald Press, 1981.

Estes, Kenneth W. *The Marine Officer's Guide*. 6th edition. Annapolis, MD: Naval Institute Press, 1996.

Falls, Thomas B. *The Writings of Saint Justin Martyr*. New York: Christian Heritage, Inc., 1948.

Ferguson, Everett. "Did You Know." *Christian History* 27 (1990): inside front cover.

Frothingham, Arthur L. "Bolshevism." *Handbook of War Facts and Peace Problems*, 4. 1919. Database on-line. Available from http://www.lib.byu.edu/~rdh/wwi/comment/WarFacts/wfacts6.htm; Internet.

Gamble, Harry Y. *The New Testament Canon: Its Making and Meaning*. Philadelphia: Fortress Press, 1985.

Giblin, Charles Homer. *The Book of Revelation: The Open Book of Prophecy*. Collegeville, Minnesota: The Liturgical Press, 1991.

Hays, Richard B. *The Moral Vision of the New Testament: Community, Cross, New Creation: A Contemporary Introduction to New Testament Ethics*. United States of America: HarperSanFrancisco, 1996.

Howe, Julia W. "The Battle Hymn of the Republic." Database on-line. Available from http://www.cyberhymnal.org/htm/b/h/bhymnotr.htm; Internet.

Holmes, Michael W., ed. *The Apostolic Fathers: Second Edition*. Trans. J.B. Lightfoot and J.R. Harmer. Grand Rapids, Michigan: Baker Book House, 1989.

The Hymnal for Worship & Celebration. Waco, Texas: Word Music, 1986.

Johnson, James Turner. "Just War, As It Was and Is." *First Things* 149 (January 2005): 23.

Jones, Peter. *The Gnostic Empire Strikes Back*. Phillipsburg, NJ: P&R Publishing, 1992.

Bibliography

Josephus, Flavius. *Jewish Antiquities.* Translated by Ralph Marcus. Vol. 7, *Books XII-XIV.* Cambridge, MA: Harvard University Press, 1943.

King, Dr. Martin Luther, Jr. "Letter from Birmingham Jail." April 16, 1963. Database on-line. Available from http://www.quotationspage.com/quote/24974.html; Internet.

Larkin, Clarence. *The Book of Revelation.* Glenside, PA: Rev. Clarence Larkin Estate, 1919.

Lewis, C. S. *The Lion, the Witch, and the Wardrobe.* New York: Collier Books, 1974.

Lincoln, Abraham. "Second Inaugural Address," 1863.

MacPherson, David. *The Incredible Cover-Up, The True Story of the Pre-Trib Rapture.* Plainfield, New Jersey: Logos International, 1975.

Marine Battle Skills Training Handbook: Book 1, PVT-CAPT, General Military Subjects *With User's Guide.* Arlington, VA: Marine Corps Institute, August 1995.

Macciavelli, Niccolo. *The Prince.* Translated by George Bull. United States of America: Penguin Books, 1982.

Morris, Leon. *The Revelation of St. John: An Introduction and Commentary.* Grand Rapids: William B. Eerdmans Publishing Company, 1978.

Mounce, Robert. *The Book of Revelation.* Grand Rapids, Michigan: Wm. B. Eerdmans Publishing Co., 1977.

Niebuhr, H. R. *Christ and Culture.* New York: Harper & Row, Publishers, Inc., 1951.

Parade, The Sunday Newspaper Magazine. (May 7, 2000): 7.

Pilgrim, Walter E. *Uneasy Neighbors: Church and State in the New Testament.* Fortress Press, 1999.

Reapsome, James. "Persecuted Christians Today." *Christian History* 27 (1990): 37.

Rist, Martin. *The Modern Reader's Guide to the Book of Revelation.* New York: Association Press, 1961.

Rosenthall, Marvin. *The Lamb That Will Roar Like a Lion.* Orlando, FL: Zion's Hope, Inc., Cassette.

Scofield, C.I., ed. *Oxford NIV Scofield Study Bible*. New York: Oxford University Press, 1984.

Smith, Robert H. *Apocalypse: A Commentary on Revelation in Words and Images*. Illustrations by Albrecht Durer. Collegeville, Minnesota: The Liturgical Press, 2000.

Tertullian, *Apologeticus*.

U.S. Department of State. "America Must Remain Engaged," 21 December 1992. *Dispatch*, vol. 3, no. 51.

Walvoord, John. *The Bible Knowledge Commentary, New Testament*. Wheaton, Illinois: Victor Books, 1986.

Walzer, Michael. *Just and Unjust Wars: A Moral Argument with Historical Illustrations*. New York: Basic Books, Inc., Publishers, 1977.

Wengst, Klaus. *Pax Romana and the Peace of Jesus Christ*. Philadelphia: Fortress Press, 1987.

Wiersbe, Warren W. *Be Victorious*. Wheaton, Illinois: Victor Books, 1985.

Wilcock, Michael. *I Saw Heaven Opened, The Message of Revelation*. Downers Grove, Illinois: InterVarsity Press, 1975.

Wills, Gary. Review of *Arguing About War*, by Michael Walzer. *The New York Review of Books* 51 (November 18, 2004).

About the Author

Roger VanDerWerken is an ordained minister with the American Baptist Churches, USA, and a chaplain in the United States Navy. He is a graduate of Schoharie Central High School in upstate New York; and holds a Bachelor of Science from the U.S. Naval Academy in Annapolis, MD; a Master of Divinity from the Westminster Theological Seminary in Philadelphia, PA; and a Master of Theology in ethics from the Jesuit School of Theology in Berkeley, CA. He has served as a surface warfare officer in the United States Navy; as an associate pastor of the First Baptist Church in Glenside, PA; and as the senior pastor of the Memorial Baptist Church in Cortland, NY. As a navy chaplain, he has been with the Marines of the First Marine Division at Camp Pendleton, CA, and is currently assigned to the aircraft carrier USS RONALD REAGAN home ported in San Diego, CA. Roger has also authored *Code of Conduct for Servants of the Most High God*, (Selah Publishing Group, 2002). He and his wife Jacque have been married for twenty-three years. They have three children, Christina (22), Beth (19), and Jordan (17). The VanDerWerken's currently reside in Oceanside, CA.

To order additional copies of
Captain's on the Bridge
have your credit card ready and call
1 800-917-BOOK (2665)

or e-mail
orders@selahbooks.com

or order online at
www.selahbooks.com

Printed in the United States
69829LV00002B/166-249